APPALACHIAN TRAIL GUIDE TO PENNSYLVANIA

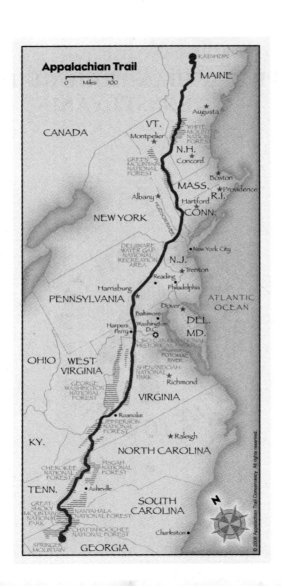

GUIDE TO

THE APPALACHIAN TRAIL
IN
PENNSYLVANIA

Number 5 of a Series

Wayne E. Gross
Editor

ELEVENTH EDITION

KEYSTONE TRAILS ASSOCIATION
Harrisburg, PA

2009

Cover Photo: **Round Head © Thomas Scully**
Inside Cover
Photo: **Pinnacle © Jeff Mitchell**

ISBN: 978-0-9717445-5-4
Eleventh Edition
Printed in the United States of America

DEDICATION

The eleventh edition is dedicated to the many volunteers of the Pennsylvania Appalachian Trail maintaining clubs for their countless hours of trail building, maintenance, shelter construction, blazing, and corridor monitoring in addition to writing newsletters, serving as officers, organizing meetings, planning programs, and leading hikes. Thanks!

**PRESERVING PENNSYLVANIA'S
FOOTPATHS SINCE 1956**

CONTENTS

NOTICE TO ALL TRAIL USERS

The information contained in this publication is the result of the best effort of the publisher, using information available to it at the time of printing. Changes resulting from maintenance work and relocations are constantly occurring and, therefore, no published route can be regarded as precisely accurate at the time you read this notice.

Notices of pending relocations are indicated. Maintenance of the Trail is conducted by volunteers and the maintaining clubs listed in this guidebook. Questions about the exact route of the Trail should be addressed to the Editor, *Appalachian Trail Guide to Pennsylvania,* Keystone Trails Association, 101 North Front Street, Harrisburg PA 17101; 717-238-7017; ktahike@verizon.net. Please pay close attention to and follow the white blazes and any directional signs.

PREFACE

It is comforting to know there is a place that we can retreat to from the bustle and stress of life. There is a place to renew our spirit and faith. There is a place where Scout and youth groups go to test their character and build self-esteem. There is a place that can help build physical and mental fitness. There is a place where our young and young at heart can go to explore our natural world. There is a place where a person can go to set a goal to hike the distance or walk a short stroll. There is a place where camaraderie is found among trail builders and maintainers in the laughter around a campfire at setting sun with the contentment of a job well done. That place was dreamed, planned, and built by prior generations. We continue the work to preserve that special place in our world for future generations. That place is the Appalachian Trail.

To the many volunteers who make the Appalachian Trail the world's premier hiking trail and on behalf of the millions who walk its path - Thanks!

This edition builds on the work of the previous editors and volunteers. This edition utilizes the unidirectional format adopted by the Appalachian Trail Conservancy. The format parallels the work done by Maurice Forrester, the previous editor.

I am indebted to the many contributors of the eleven trail maintaining clubs in Pennsylvania and other helpers. They are listed in the acknowledgements section. They have assisted with this project in addition to their other volunteer duties.

Many of the photographs are from fellow trail volunteers in the maintaining clubs of Pennsylvania. Enjoy these snapshots of the A.T.

The sketches are the work of Robert Miller, a talented young man, who I first met in Scouting while producing a Where To Go Camping guide.

Corrections can be sent to the editor in care of the Keystone Trails Association and to the local maintaining club for that section. Your help is appreciated.

May you enjoy great adventures hiking the Appalachian Trail in the Keystone State as it unfolds in the following pages.

Wayne E. Gross
Canadensis, PA
March, 2009

ACKNOWLEDGMENTS

The team of field editors, who perform the basic task of collecting the raw data from which the trail descriptions are built, represent the crucial linchpin, without which everything else would fall apart. This guidebook could not be produced without their help. Listed from north to south according to their Trail maintenance responsibilities, they are:

Wilmington Trail Club: Mike Kintner and William Tinney
BATONA Hiking Club: Edward Schellhase, Paul Piechoski, and Allen Britton
Appalachian Mountain Club, Delaware Valley Chapter: Daniel Schwartz
Philadelphia Trail Club: David Scheid
Allentown Hiking Club: Ed Ritter
Blue Mountain Eagle Climbing Club: Scott Birchman
Susquehanna A.T. Club: Thomas Scully
York Hiking Club: James Hooper
Mountain Club of Maryland: Paul Ives
Cumberland Valley A.T. Club: Frank Bohn and James Foster
Potomac A.T. Club, North Chapter: James Stauch, Jr.

Brian King, Karen Lutz, John Luthy, Michelle Miller, Robert Sickley, Kathleen Mallow-Sager, Laurie Potteiger and other staff members of the Appalachian Trail Conservancy provided assistance and comments.

Various agencies of Pennsylvania State Government provided a wealth of information that has been incorporated in this book. The Pennsylvania Game Commission; the Bureau of Forestry; and the Bureau of State Parks all provided comments and advice. Thank you to Mary Linkevich of Hawk Mountain Sanctuary for her assistance and thanks to Richard Martin for his revisions to the Pennsylvania geology section.

The sketches are the work of Robert Miller and may not be copied or reused without his written permission. The photographs are the work of Allen Britton, James Foster, Wayne E. Gross, Jeff Mitchell, Charles Olge, Lorrie Preston, David Scheid, Thomas Scully,

James Stauch, Jr., and Ernest Yeagley. The photographs may not be reproduced without written permission from the photographer.

Thanks to Shirley Gross for her assistance and Barbara Wiemann, John Luthy and Frank Allen for their proofreading efforts.

For my family's and friends' support and patience - Thank you.

Finally. thank you to all those who helped in a variety of ways but whose names I have failed to note here.

USING THE GUIDE

This Guide is Number Five of a series of guidebooks describing the entire Appalachian Trail from Maine to Georgia. The other books in the series are listed on the back cover.

The book is organized with general and background material at the beginning. Included in this section is information on the history of the Appalachian Trail, the Appalachian Trail Conservancy, Keystone Trails Association, the nature of the Trail and land ownership in Pennsylvania, and general information for the assistance of hikers.

About half of the Guide consists of detailed trail description. The Trail in Pennsylvania is divided into fourteen sections of varying lengths. Trail information is given for each section, with general material listed first, followed by detailed description in columnar format with mileage for North to South and South to North listed simultaneously.

In preparing this guidebook it is assumed that hikers will supply themselves with the Trail maps published by Keystone Trails Association. For the Trail south of the Susquehanna River, the maps are published by the Potomac Appalachian Trail Club. Most automobile road maps, as well as the Pennsylvania Official Transportation Map, show the route of the Appalachian Trail. These can be useful in determining the main highway crossings. A copy of the Official Pennsylvania Map can be obtained without charge by writing to: Pennsylvania Department of Transportation, Harrisburg, PA 17120.

INTRODUCTION
ABOUT THE
APPALACHIAN TRAIL

Welcome to the America's best-known long-distance footpath, the Appalachian Trail. If you've never visited it before, you're in for a memorable time, and we hope this official guidebook will help you make the most of it. If you know the Trail, but not this part of it, we hope this book will help you discover new aspects of an experience that changes from state to state, mile to mile, and season to season.

Not long after the end of World War I, a Massachusetts forester and dreamer named Benton MacKaye publicly envisioned a footpath running along the crests of the eastern mountains, from New England to the southern Appalachians. The work of scores of volunteers helped that dream become the Appalachian Trail, which, extended more than 2,178 miles between Katahdin, in central Maine, and Springer Mountain, in northern Georgia. Its terrain ranges from swampland bog bridges to near-vertical rock scrambles that challenge the fittest wilderness trekker; its white blazes lead from busy small-town streets to remote mountain ridges, days from the nearest road crossing.

The "A.T.," as it's called by hikers, is a linear trail that can be enjoyed in small pieces or large chunks. Hikers follow its blazes on round-trip day-hikes, on loop-hikes (where side-trails connect with it and form a loop), on one-way section-hikes, on overnight backpacking trips that cover short or long segments, or on end-to-end "thru-hikes" that cover the entire Trail. It is continuously marked, using a standard system of paint blazes and signs, and is cleared of undergrowth and maintained to permit single-file hiking. (Bicycles, horses, and motorized vehicles are not permitted along almost all of the route.) Many campsites and more than 250 primitive woodland shelters are located along the Trail, typically about a day's hike apart. The path itself is usually dirt, or rock, or grass, and only very short segments are paved or wheelchair-accessible.

This remarkable footpath is much more than just a walk through the woods. When it was first begun in the 1920s and completed in the 1930s, it was little-known and rarely traveled. Large parts of it were on private property. Since 1968, it has been a part of the same national park system that includes Yellowstone, Yosemite, and the Great Smoky Mountains. Its official name today is the Appalachian National Scenic Trail, and more than 99 percent of it runs over public lands. Hundreds of roads cross it, and hundreds of side trails intersect with it. In some parts, the Trail "corridor" is only a few hundred feet wide; in other parts, entire mountains are encompassed by it.

Unlike other well-known national parks, there's no "main entrance" to the A.T., with a gate and a ranger collecting tickets. You can begin or end your hike at hundreds of places between its northern and southern ends. As the longest, skinniest unit of America's, the A.T. stretches across fourteen states and passes through more than sixty federal, state, and local parks and forests. Maybe the most important difference between the A.T. and other national-park units, though, is that it was built by volunteers, and volunteers still are responsible for keeping it up. The A.T. relies on a system known as "cooperative management" rather than on a large, paid federal staff. Yes, a handful of National Park Service staff members are assigned to the Appalachian Trail Park Office in Harpers Ferry, West Virginia, but thousands of the people who maintain, patrol, and monitor the footpath and its surrounding lands are outdoor lovers like you. Each year, as members of thirty "maintaining clubs" up and down the Appalachians, they volunteer hundreds of thousands of hours of their time looking after this public treasure. They would welcome your help.

About the Appalachian Trail Conservancy - We are the volunteer-based organization that manages the public land through which the Trail passes, teaches people about the Trail, coordinates the work of the maintaining clubs, and works with the government agencies, individuals, and companies that own the land t. the Trail passes over or near. The membership of the Appalachian Trail Conservancy (ATC) includes more than 35,000 hikers and Trail enthusiasts, who elect a volunteer board every two years. Members' contributions help support a paid staff of about 45 people at the ATC headquarters in Harpers Ferry, West Virginia, and at field offices in New England, Pennsylvania, Virginia, andNorth Carolina. Our Web site, www.appalachiantrail.org, is a good source of information about the Trail. Information about contacting the Conservancy is elsewhere in this guide. Please support our conservation work by becoming a member.

Volunteer Trail maintainers

HOW TO USE THIS BOOK

We suggest that you use this book in conjunction with the waterproof Trail maps that were sold with it. Certain maps can be purchased separately from the guidebooks, but not for all sections of the Trail. Information about services available in towns near the Trail is updated annually in the *Appalachian Trail Thru-Hikers' Companion*. Mileage and shelter information for the entire Trail is updated annually in the *Appalachian Trail Data Book*, available from ATC. Check the ATC website (www.appalachiantrail.org) for the latest Trail Updates and *Appalachian Trail Thru-Hikers' Companion* updates.

Although the Trail is usually well-marked, and experienced hikers may be able to follow it without either guidebook or map, using the book and the maps will not only help keep you from getting lost or disoriented but will also help you get more out of your hike.

Before you start your hike:

• *Decide where you want to go and which Trail features you hope to see.* Use the book to help you plan your trip. The introductions to each section give more detail, summarizing scenic and cultural highlights that you may wish to visit along the route.

• *Calculate mileage for linear or loop hikes.* Each chapter lists mileage between landmarks on the route, along with details to help you follow the path. Use the mileage and descriptions to determine how far you must hike, how long it will take you, and where you can camp if you're taking an overnight or long-distance hike.

• *Find the Trail.* Use the road access descriptions in the guidebook to locate parking areas near the A.T. and the "Trailheads" or "road crossings" where the footpath crosses the highway. In some cases, the guidebook includes directions to nearby towns and commercial areas where you can find food, supplies, and lodging. Check the ATC website www.appalachiantrail.org for the latest information on Trailhead parking, including any reports of vandalism.

After you begin hiking:

• *Identify landmarks.* Deduce where you are along the Trail by comparing the descriptions in the guidebook and the features on the waterproof maps to the landscape you're hiking through. Much of the time, the Trail's blazes will lead you through seemingly featureless woodlands, where the only thing you can see in most directions is trees, but periodically you will be able to check your progress at viewpoints, meadows, mountain tops, stream crossings, road crossings, and Trailside structures.

• *Learn about the route.* Native Americans, colonial-era settlers, Civil War soldiers, nineteenth-century farmers, pioneering railroaders, and early industrial entrepreneurs explored these hills long before the A.T. was built. Although much of what they left behind has long since been abandoned and overgrown, your guidebook will point out old settlements and forest roads and put the landscape in its historical context. It will touch on the geology, natural history, and modern-day ecosystems of the eastern mountains.

• *Find campsites and side trails.* The guidebook includes directions to other trails, as well as creeks, mountain springs, and established tenting and shelter sites.

Areas covered

Each of the eleven official Appalachian Trail guidebooks describes several hundred miles of the Trail. In some cases, that includes a single state, such as Maine or Pennsylvania. In other cases, the guidebook may include several states, such as the one covering northern Virginia, West Virginia, and Maryland. Because so much of the Trail is in Virginia (more than 500 miles of it), a hiker needs to use four different guidebooks to cover that entire state.

The eleven guidebooks are:

Maine
New Hampshire–Vermont
Massachusetts–Connecticut
New York–New Jersey
Pennsylvania
Maryland and Northern Virginia
Shenandoah National Park
Central Virginia
Southwest Virginia
Tennessee–North Carolina
North Carolina–Georgia

How the guidebook is divided

Rather than trying to keep track of the Trail from beginning to end, the Trail's maintainers break it down into smaller "sections." Each section typically covers the area between important road crossings or natural features and can vary from three to thirty miles in length. A typical section is from five to fifteen miles long. This guidebook is organized according to those sections, beginning with the northernmost in the coverage area and ending with the southernmost. Each section makes up a chapter. A summary of distances for the entire guidebook appears on pages 70 to 72.

How chapters are organized

Brief description of section - Each chapter begins with a brief description of the route. The description mentions highlights and prominent features and gives a sense of what it's like to hike the section as a whole.

Section map and profile - The map shows how to find the Trail from your car (it is not a detailed map and should not be relied on for navigating the Trail) and includes notable roads along with a rough depiction of the Trail route, showing shelter locations. A schematic profile of the high and low points in the section gives you an idea of how much climbing or descending is ahead.

Shelters and campsites - Each chapter also includes an overview of shelters and campsites for the section, including the distances between shelters and information about water supplies. Along some parts of the Trail, particularly north of the Mason-Dixon Line, the designated sites are the only areas in which camping is permitted. In other parts of the Trail, even where "dispersed camping" is allowed, we recommend that hikers "Leave No Trace" and reduce their impact on the Trail's resources by using established campsites. If camping is restricted in a section, it will be noted here.

Trail description - Trail descriptions appear on the both sides of the pages of each chapter. Although the description reads from north to south, it is organized for both northbound and southbound hikers. Northbound hikers should start at the end of the chapter and read up, using the mileages in the right-hand column. Southbound hikers should read down, using the mileages in the left-hand column. The description includes obvious landmarks you will pass, although it may not include all stream crossings, summits, or side trails. Where the Trail route becomes confusing, the guide will provide both north- and southbound directions from the landmark. When a feature appears in **bold** type, it means that you should see the section highlights for more detail.

Section highlights - On the left-hand pages of each chapter, you will find cultural, historical, natural, and practical information about the bold items in the Trail description. That includes detailed information about Trailheads, shelters, and campsites, along with notes on the historical and cultural resources of the route, notes on landforms and natural history, and descriptions of side trails.

Guidebook conventions

North or "compass-north"? - For the sake of convenience, the directions north, south, east and west in the guide refer to the general north–south orientation of the Trail, rather than the true north or magnetic north of maps and charts. In other words, when a hiker is northbound on the Trail, whatever is to his left will be referred to as "west" and whatever is to the right will be "east." For south bounders, the opposite is true.

Although this is instinctively the way A.T. hikers orient themselves, it can be slightly confusing for the first-time A.T. hiker, since the Trail does not always follow an actual north–south orientation. For example, you might be "northbound" along the Trail (headed toward Maine), but, because of a sharp turn or a switchback up the side of a mountain, your compass will tell you you're actually pointed south for several miles. Nevertheless, in this guide, a trail or road intersecting on the left side of the A.T. for the northbound hiker will always be referred to as "intersecting on the west side of the A.T.," even where the compass says otherwise.

When the compass direction of an object is important, as when directing attention to a certain feature seen from a viewpoint, the guidebook will refer to "compass-north," "compass-west," and so forth.

Undocumented features - The separate waterproof hiking maps meant to accompany this guide generally reflect all the landmarks discussed here. Because the maps are extremely detailed, some features that appear on them, such as streams and old woods roads, may not be mentioned in the guidebook if they are not important landmarks. Other side trails that the hiker encounters may not be mentioned or mapped at all; in general, this is because the unmarked trails lead onto private property, and Trail managers wish to discourage their use.

TIPS FOR ENJOYING THE
APPALACHIAN TRAIL

Follow the blazes - The Appalachian Trail is marked for daylight travel in both directions, using a system of paint "blazes" on trees, posts, and rocks. There are some local variations, but most hikers grasp the system quickly. Above treeline, and where snow or fog may obscure paint marks, posts and rock piles called "cairns" are used to identify the route.

A blaze is a rectangle of paint in a prominent place along a trail. White-paint blazes two inches wide and six inches high mark the A.T. itself. Side trails and shelter trails use blue blazes; blazes of other colors and shapes mark intersecting trails. Two white blazes, one above the other, signal an obscure turn, route change, incoming side trail, or other situation that requires you to be especially alert to changes in direction. In some areas, the upper blaze of the two blazes will be offset in the direction of the turn.

If you have gone a quarter-mile without seeing a blaze, stop. Retrace your steps until you locate a blaze. Then, check to ensure that you haven't missed a turn. Often a glance backward will reveal blazes meant for hikers traveling in the opposite direction.

White blaze

Double blaze

Volunteer Trail maintainers regularly relocate small sections of the path around hazards or undesirable features or off private property. When your map or guidebook indicates one route, and the blazes show another, follow the blazes.

A few cautions - The A.T. is a scenic trail through the forests of the Appalachian Mountains. It is full of natural splendors and is fun to hike, and parts of it run near roads and across fairly level ground. But most of the Trail is very steep and runs deep in the woods, along the crests of rocky mountain ridges, miles from the nearest houses or paved roads. It will test your physical conditioning and skills. Plan your hike, and prepare sensibly.

Before you set out to hike the Trail, take a few minutes to review the information in this guidebook. It is as current as possible, but conditions and footpath locations sometimes change in between guidebook editions. The ATC website (www.appalachiantrail.org) can be checked for the latest Trail Updates. On the Trail, please pay close attention to—and follow—the blazes and any directional signs that mark the route, even if the book describes a different route.

Although we have included some basic tips for preparing for an A.T. hike in this guidebook, this is not a "how-to" guide to backpacking. Many good books of that sort are available at your local bookstore, outfitter, and library. If you've never hiked before, we recommend that you take the time to read one or two and to research equipment, camping techniques, and trip planning.

Post

Cairn

If your only hiking and camping experience is in local parks and forests, be aware that hiking and camping in the mountains can be extremely strenuous and disorienting and has its own particular challenges. You will sometimes encounter wildlife and will have to make do with primitive (or nonexistent) sanitary facilities. Remember that water in the backcountry, even at water sources mentioned in this guidebook, needs to be treated for microorganisms before you drink it.

Responsibility for safety - Finally, know that you are responsible for your own safety, for the safety of those with you, and for making sure that your food and water are safe for consumption. Hiking the A.T. is no more dangerous than many other popular outdoor activities, but, although the Trail is part of the national park system, it is not the proverbial "walk in the park." The Appalachian Trail Conservancy and its member maintaining clubs cannot ensure the safety of any hiker on the Trail; as a hiker, you assume the risk for any accident, illness, or injury that might occur there.

Leave No Trace - As more and more people use the Trail and other backcountry areas, it becomes more important to learn to enjoy wild places without ruining them. The best way to do this is to understand and practice the principles of Leave No Trace, a seven-point ethic for enjoying the backcountry that applies to everything from a picnic outing to a long-distance expedition. Leave No Trace, Inc., is a nonprofit organization dedicated to teaching the principles of low-impact use. For more information, contact Leave No Trace at www.lnt.org, or call 800-332-4100.

The seven principles of the I eave No Trace ethic are:

1. **Plan ahead and prepare.** Evaluate the risks associated with your outing, identify campsites and destinations in advance, use maps and guides, and be ready for bad weather. When people don't plan ahead, they're more likely to damage the backcountry.

2. **Travel and camp on durable surfaces.** Stay on trails, and don't bushwhack short-cuts across switchbacks or other bends in the path. Keep off fragile trailside areas, such as bogs or alpine zones. Camp in designated spots, such as shelters and existing campsites, so that unspoiled areas aren't trampled and denuded.

3. **Dispose of waste properly.** Bury or pack out excrement not deposited in privies, including pet droppings. Pack out all trash and food waste, including that left behind by others. Don't bury trash or food, and don't try to burn packaging materials in campfires.

4. **Leave what you find.** Don't take flowers or other sensitive natural resources. Don't disturb artifacts such as native American arrowheads or the stone walls and cellar holes of historical woodland homesteads.

5. **Minimize campfire impacts.** Campfires are enjoyable, but they also create the worst visual and ecological impact of any backcountry camping practice. If possible, cook on a backpacking stove instead of a fire. Where fires are permitted, build them only in established fire rings, and don't add rocks to an existing ring. Keep fires small. Burn only dead and downed wood that can be broken by hand—leave axes and saws at home. Never leave your campfire unattended, and drown it when you leave.

6. **Respect wildlife.** Don't feed or disturb wildlife. Store food properly to avoid attracting bears, varmints, and rodents. If you bring a pet, keep it leashed.

7. **Be considerate of other visitors.** Limit overnight groups to ten or fewer; twenty-five on day trips. Minimize noise and intrusive behavior. Share shelters and other facilities. Be considerate of Trail neighbors.

ABBREVIATIONS

A.T.	Appalachian Trail
AHC	Allentown Hiking Club
AMC-DV	Appalachian Mountain Club – Delaware Valley Chapter
ATC	Appalachian Trail Conservancy
AYH	American Youth Hostel
BATONA	BATONA Hiking Club (Back to Nature)
BMECC	Blue Mountain Eagle Climbing Club
CVATC	Cumberland Valley Appalachian Trail Club
ft.	Foot/Feet
KTA	Keystone Trails Association
MCM	Mountain Club of Maryland
mi.	Mile(s)
NPS	National Park Service
NRA	National Recreation Area
PTC	Philadelphia Trail Club
PATC	Potomac Appalachian Trail Club
PennDOT	Pennsylvania Department of Transportation
Rt.	Route
SATC	Susquehanna Appalachian Trail Club
USGS	U.S. Geological Survey
WTC	Wilmington Trail Club
yds	Yard(s)
YHC	York Hiking Club

MILES TO KILOMETERS
CONVERSION TABLE

	0.0	1.0	2.0	3.0	4.0
0.0	0.000	1.609	3.219	4.828	6.437
0.1	0.161	1.770	3.380	4.989	6.598
0.2	0.322	1.931	3.541	5.150	6.759
0.3	0.483	2.092	3.702	5.311	6.920
0.4	0.644	2.253	3.862	5.472	7.081
0.5	0.805	2.414	4.023	5.633	7.242
0.6	0.966	2.575	4.184	5.794	7.403
0.7	1.127	2.736	4.345	5.955	7.564
0.8	1.288	2.897	4.506	6.116	7.725
0.9	1.449	3.058	4.667	6.277	7.886

	5.0	6.0	7.0	8.0	9.0	10.0
0.0	8.047	9.656	11.266	12.875	14.484	16.094
0.1	8.208	9.817	11.426	13.036	14.645	16.254
0.2	8.369	9.978	11.587	13.197	14.806	16.415
0.3	8.530	10.139	11.748	13.358	14.967	16.576
0.4	8.691	10.300	11.909	13.519	15.128	16.737
0.5	8.851	10.461	12.070	13.680	15.289	16.898
0.6	9.012	10.622	12.231	13.840	15.450	17.059
0.7	9.173	19.783	12.392	14.001	15.611	17.220
0.8	9.334	10.944	12.553	14.162	15.772	17.381
0.9	9.495	11.105	12.714	14.323	15.933	17.542

EXAMPLE: To convert 7.4 miles to kilometers.

(1) Find the mile column labeled "7.0"

(2) Find the "tenth" row for that column labeled "0.4"

The intersection of the mile column and the tenth row will give you the conversion to kilometers, in this case, 11.909 km.

0.01 Miles = .0161 km.

KEYSTONE TRAILS ASSOCIATION

Preserving Pennsylvania's Footpaths

Keystone Trails Association (KTA), a volunteer-directed, public service organization, is an alliance of member organizations and individuals dedicated to providing, preserving, protecting and promoting recreational hiking trails and hiking opportunities in Pennsylvania, and to representing and advocating the interests and concerns of the Pennsylvania hiking community. Founded in 1956, KTA, through the quarterly newsletter and its website (www.kta-hike.org), informs members and hikers about hiking-related activities.

The objectives of KTA as set forth in its bylaws are:

*Coordinate the efforts of walking and hiking groups in and around Pennsylvania;

*Develop, build, and maintain hiking trails, including trail support facilities;

*Protect hiking trail lands through support and advocacy, as well as by acquisition when desirable and feasible; and

*Educate the public in the responsible use of trails and the natural environment.

In addition to this guidebook and the map set, KTA publishes *Pennsylvania Hiking Trails*, which offers a diverse array of hiking experiences, from backcountry treks to leisurely rambles that highlight the state's natural beauty and unique geography. Directions, trailhead locations, hiking times, maintenance updates, and points of interest are included. Visit the KTA website to view other maps and books that are available for sale.

The KTA volunteer trail care and maintenance group offers volunteers the opportunity to participate for a day, a weekend or for a six day stretch at various locations in the state. All skill levels are welcome. Check the KTA website for details.

KTA sponsors Pennsylvania Hiking Week each spring with over 100 guided hikes led by experienced leaders in cooperation with the Pennsylvania Department of Conservation and Natural Resources. Other hiking activities include a 25-mile challenge Super Hike and a weekend of guided hiking in Sproul State forest.

KTA holds a spring and fall membership meeting each year, open to the public, which include guided hiking programs, at various locations across the state. The fall meeting includes an awards program for hikers achieving the completion of various trails in the state.

All of KTA's activities are open to the public, but for those who would like to become members, please go to www.kta-hike.org for more information. KTA also welcomes member organizations that may be interested in affiliating with KTA.

Thyra Sperry, President
Curt Ashenfelter, Executive Director

KEYSTONE TRAILS ASSOCIATION
101 North Front Street
Harrisburg, PA 17101
Telephone: 717-238-7017
http://www.kta-hike.org
ktaadmin@verizon.net

THE APPALACHIAN TRAIL CONSERVANCY

The Appalachian Trail Conservancy (ATC) is a volunteer-based, nonprofit corporation organization dedicated to the preservation and management of the natural, scenic, historic, and cultural resources associated with the Appalachian National Scenic Trail in order to provide primitive outdoor-recreation and educational opportunities for Trail visitors. ATC coordinates the efforts of trail clubs, state and local governments, the National Park Service, and individuals in trail management and maintenance. The Conservancy publishes booklets of various types and guidebooks for many A.T. sections. Guide books for all sections (whether published by ATC or others) are available from the ATC office and ATC website. In addition, the Conservancy supplies information on the construction and maintenance of hiking trails and general information on hiking and trail use.

The membership of the Conservancy is made up of organizations which maintain the Trail or contribute to the Trail project, individuals who in either personal or official capacity are responsible for the maintenance of sections of the Trail, and individual dues-paying members.

ATC membership includes a subscription to *A.T. Journeys*, published six times a year. The Conservancy's website also features a bi-monthly newsletter, *The Register*, written primarily for Trail maintainers. Guidebooks, maps, and a variety of other publications for hikers and the general public are also available at discounted prices to ATC members. Membership application material, and a complete list of publications, with current prices, are available from the Conservancy's website or by writing to the address below.

The Conservancy's headquarters is located at 799 Washington Street in Harpers Ferry, WV. The A.T. Visitor Center is open seven days a week from 9-5.

Contact:

> **APPALACHIAN TRAIL CONSERVANCY**
> PO Box 807
> Harpers Ferry, WV 25425-0807
> Phone 304-535-6331
> www.appalachiantrail.org
> info@appalachiantrail.org

ATC's Mid-Atlantic Regional Office is located on the A.T. overlooking Children's Lake in Boiling Springs, PA. Trail information is provided by staff members during office hours, 8:00 A.M. to 3:30 P.M. weekdays. The office also has a small shop offering ATC memberships, guidebooks, maps, and associated items for sale. Hiker information and the Trail register are always available on the office's front porch.

Contact:

> **APPALACHIAN TRAIL CONSERVANCY**
> 4 East First Street
> PO Box 625
> Boiling Springs, PA 17007
> Phone 717-258-5771
> atc-maro@appalachiantrail.org

QUESTIONS AND ANSWERS
ABOUT THE
APPALACHIAN TRAIL

Preparation

Proper planning and preparation will make your Trail experience easier, safer, and more enjoyable. ATC's website and publications provide a wealth of information to assist you during your planning process.

What should I carry?

The A.T. is enjoyable to hike, but inexperienced hikers - even those just out for an hour or two - can quickly find themselves deep in the woods, on steep terrain, and in wet, chilly conditions. Carrying a basic "kit" helps hikers cope with such situations.

Packing for a day-hike is relatively simple:

> Map and compass (learn to use them first!)
> Water (at least 2–3 quarts)
> Warm clothing and rain gear
> Food (including extra high-energy snacks)
> Trowel (to bury human waste) and toilet paper
> First-aid kit, with blister treatments
> Whistle (three blasts is the international signal for help)
> Garbage bag (to carry out trash)
> Flashlight (with extra batteries and bulb)

On longer hikes, especially in remote or rugged terrain, add:

> Heavy-duty garbage bag (emergency shelter or to insulate
>   a hypothermia victim)
> Sharp knife
> Fire starter (a candle, for instance) and waterproof matches

If you're backpacking and plan to camp out, we suggest you consult a good "how-to" book for details about what to carry or talk to an experienced hiker. Visit the ATC website for the free, downloadable booklet *Step by Step: An Introduction to Walking the Appalachian Trail*. Although we don't have room here to discuss gear in detail, most A.T. backpackers carry the following items, in addition to the day-hike checklist. Some of the items can be shared with a partner to lighten the load:

Shelter (a tent or tarp)
Lightweight pot, cooking utensils
Stove (a small backpacking model, with fuel)
Medium-sized backpack (big "expedition-size" packs
    are usually overkill)
A pack cover or plastic bag (to keep gear dry in rainy weather)
Sleeping pad (to insulate you from the cold ground)
Sleeping bag of appropriate warmth for the season
Food and clothing
Rope or cord (to hang your food at night)
Water filter, iodine tablets, or another method of treating water

Where can I park?

Park in designated areas. Many of them will be indicated in the Trailhead entries for this guidebook and may be marked on Trail maps. If you leave your car overnight unattended, however, you risk theft or vandalism. Many hikers avoid this worry by arranging for a "shuttle" to drop them off at a Trailhead or arranging to leave their car in the parking lot of a business located near the Trail; ask first, and offer to pay a little something to the business. Some sections of the Trail are served by public transportation. If you decide to park at a Trailhead, hide your property and valuables from sight, or, better yet, leave them at home, so they do not inspire a thief to break in and steal them. Check ATC's website for the current list of shuttlers, and for parking tips at every Trailhead including any reports of vandalism.

Using the Trail

Where and how do I find water?

Year-round natural water sources are listed in this guidebook; springs and streams are marked on most official A.T. maps. Most (although not all) shelters are near a year-round water source. Some springs and streams dry up during late summer and early fall.

Is the water safe to drink?
Water in the backcountry and in water sources along the A.T. can be contaminated by microorganisms, including giardia lamblia and others that cause diarrhea or stomach problems. We recommend that you treat all water, using a filter or purifier or water-treatment tablets, or by boiling it.

Are there rest rooms?
Many A.T. shelters have privies, but usually you will need to "go in the woods." Proper disposal of human (and pet) waste is not only a courtesy to other hikers, but a vital Leave No Trace practice for maintaining healthy water supplies in the backcountry and an enjoyable hiking experience for others. No one should venture onto the A.T. without a trowel, used for digging a "cathole" 6"–8" deep to bury waste. Bury feces at least two hundred feet or seventy paces away from water, trails, or shelters. Use a stick to mix dirt with your waste, which hastens decomposition and discourages animals from digging it up. Used toilet paper should either be buried in your cathole or carried out in a sealed plastic bag. Hygiene products such as sanitary napkins should always be carried out.

Can I wash up in a mountain stream or spring?
Please don't. Carry water from the water source in a bottle or other container, and then wash your dishes, and yourself, at least 70 paces away from streams, springs, and ponds. Don't leave food scraps to rot in water sources, and don't foul them with products such as detergent, toothpaste, and human or animal waste.

Are bikes allowed on the Trail?
Bikes are allowed only where the Appalachian Trail shares the route with the C&O Towpath in Maryland, the Virginia Creeper Trail in the vicinity of Damascus, Virginia, roads in towns, and on certain bridges. They are not permitted on most of the Trail.

Can I bring my dog?
Yes, except where dogs are prohibited (in Great Smoky Mountains National Park, Bear Mountain Zoo, and Baxter State Park). Dogs must be leashed on National Park Service lands and on many state park and forest lands. ATC's World Wide Web site, www.appalachiantrail.org, offers details about hiking with dogs. Although dogs can be wonderful hiking companions, they can create many problems for other hikers and wildlife if you don't control

them. If taken, they should not be allowed to run free; leashing at all times is strongly recommended. Keep dogs out of springs and shelters and away from other hikers, their food, and their gear. Not all dogs can stand the wear and tear of a long hike.

How about horses, llamas, or other pack stock?
Horses are not allowed on the A.T., except where the Appalachian Trail coincides for about three miles with the C&O Canal Towpath in Maryland and on about 50 percent of the A.T. in the Smokies (where, by law, the route is open for horses as a historical use). Llamas and other pack animals are not allowed on the A.T., which is designed, built, and maintained for foot travel. Pack animals would seriously damage the treadway, discourage volunteer maintenance efforts, and make the Trail experience less enjoyable for other hikers.

Are any fees required to hike the A.T.?
No. However, there are entrance fees to some of the national parks the Trail passes through, as well as parking fees and campsite fees in popular areas, to help pay for maintenance costs.

Health and safety

Is the Trail a safe place?
In general, yes. But, like many other popular recreational activities, hiking on the A.T. is not without risk. Don't let the following discussion of potential dangers alarm you or discourage you from enjoying the Trail, but remember not to leave your common sense and intuition behind when you strap on your backpack.

In an emergency, how do I get help?
Much of the A.T. is within range of mobile phone systems, although signal reception is sometimes not good in gaps, hollows, and valleys; shelters are often located in such areas of poor reception. Emergency numbers are included in this guidebook and on maps. If you don't have a phone or can't get through, the standard call for distress consists of three short calls, audible or visible, repeated at regular intervals. A whistle is particularly good for audible signals. Visible signals may include, in daytime, light flashed with a mirror or smoke puffs; at night, a flashlight or three small bright fires. Anyone recognizing such a signal should acknowledge with two calls - if possible, by the same method - then go to the distressed person to

determine the nature of the emergency. Arrange for additional aid, if necessary.

Most of the A.T. is well enough traveled that, if you are injured, you can expect to be found. However, if an area is remote and the weather is bad, fewer hikers will be on the Trail, especially after dark. As a rule, keep your pack with you, and, even in an emergency, don't leave marked trails and try to "bushwhack" out—you will be harder to find and are more likely to encounter dangerous terrain. If you must leave the Trail, study the guidebook or map carefully for the nearest place where people are likely to be and attempt to move in that direction. If it is necessary to leave a heavy pack behind, be sure to take essentials, in case your rescue is delayed. In bad weather, a night in the open without proper covering could be fatal.

What's the most dangerous aspect of hiking the A.T.?

Perhaps the most serious dangers are hypothermia, a fall on slick rocks and logs, or a sprained or broken limb far from the nearest rescue squad or pay phone. Those are also the best arguments for hiking with a partner, who can get help in an emergency.

What sort of first-aid kit should I pack?

A basic kit to take care of bruises, scrapes, skinned knees, and blisters. The following kit weighs about a pound and occupies about a 3" x 6" x 9" space: eight 4" x 4" gauze pads; four 3" x 4" gauze pads; five 2" bandages; ten 1" bandages; six alcohol prep pads; ten large butterfly closures; one triangular bandage (40"); two 3" rolls of gauze; twenty tablets of aspirin-free pain-killer; one 15' roll of 2" adhesive tape; one 3" Ace bandage; one 3" x 4" moleskin or other blister-care products; three safety pins; one small scissors; one tweezers; personal medications as necessary.

Will I encounter snakes?

Poisonous and nonpoisonous snakes are widespread along the Trail in warm weather, but they will usually be passive. Watch where you step and where you put your hands. Please, don't kill snakes! Some are federally protected under the Endangered Species Act.

What other creatures are problems for people?

Allergic reactions to bee stings can be a problem. Ticks, which carry Lyme disease, are also a risk; always check yourself for ticks daily. Poisonous spiders are sometimes found at shelters and campsites.

Mosquitoes and blackflies may plague you in some seasons. Porcupines, skunks, raccoons, and squirrels are quite common and occasionally raid shelters and well-established camping areas after dark, looking for food. Mice are permanent residents at most shelters and may carry diseases.

What about bears?

Black bears live along many parts of the Trail and are particularly common in Georgia, the Shenandoah and Great Smoky Mountains national parks, and parts of Pennsylvania and New Jersey. They are always looking for food. Bears that have lost their fear of humans may "bluff charge" to get you to drop food or a backpack. If you encounter a black bear, it will probably run away. If it does not, back away slowly, watching the bear but not making direct eye contact. Do not run away or play dead. If a bear attacks, fight for all you are worth. The best defense against bears is preparing and storing food properly. Cook and eat your meals away from your tent or shelter, so food odors do not linger. Hang your food, cookware, toothpaste, and personal-hygiene items in a sturdy bag from a strong tree branch at least ten feet off the ground, four feet from the tree and branch, and well away from your campsite.

Is poison ivy common along the A.T.?

Yes. It grows plentifully in the wild, particularly south of New England, and can be an annoyance during hiking season. If you have touched poison ivy, wash immediately with strong soap (but not with one containing added oil). If a rash develops in the next day or so, treat it with calamine lotion or Solarcaine. Do not scratch. If blisters become serious or the rash spreads to the eyes, see a doctor.

Will I catch a disease?

The most common illnesses encountered on the A.T. are water-borne, come from ingesting protozoa (such as giardia lamblia), and respond well to antibiotics. But, the Lyme-disease bacterium and other tick-borne illnesses are legitimate concerns, too; mosquito-borne illnesses such as the West Nile virus are less common in Trail states. Cases of rabies have been reported in foxes, raccoons, and other small animals; a bite is a serious concern, although instances of hikers being bitten are rare. One case of the dangerous rodent-borne disease hantavirus has been reported on the A.T. Avoid sleeping on mouse droppings (use a mat or tent) or handling mice. Treat your water, and wash your hands.

Will I encounter hazardous weather?

Walking in the open means you will be susceptible to sudden changes in the weather, and traveling on foot means that it may be hard to find shelter quickly. Pay attention to the changing skies. Sudden spells of "off-season" cold weather, hail, and even snow are common along many parts of the Trail. Winter-like weather often occurs in late spring or early fall in the southern Appalachians, Vermont, New Hampshire, and Maine. In the northern Appalachians, it can snow during any month of the year.

What are the most serious weather-related dangers?

Hypothermia, lightning, and heat exhaustion are all legitimate concerns. Don't let the fear of them ruin your hike, but take sensible precautions.

Hypothermia - A cold rain can be the most dangerous weather of all, because it can cause hypothermia (or "exposure") even when conditions are well above freezing. Hypothermia occurs when wind and rain chill the body so that its core temperature drops; death occurs if the condition is not caught in time. Avoid hypothermia by dressing in layers of synthetic clothing, eating well, staying hydrated, and knowing when to hole up in a warm sleeping bag in a tent or shelter. Cotton clothing, such as blue jeans, tends to chill you when it gets wet from rain or sweat; if the weather turns bad, cotton clothes increase your risk of hypothermia. Natural wool and artificial fibers such as nylon, polyester, and polypropylene all do a much better job of insulation in cold, wet weather. Remember that, when the wind blows, its "chill" effect can make you much colder than the temperature would lead you to suspect, especially if you're sweaty or wet.

Lightning - The odds of being struck by lightning are low, but an open ridge is no place to be during a thunderstorm. If a storm is coming, immediately leave exposed areas. Boulders, rocky overhangs, and shallow caves offer no protection from lightning, which may actually flow through them along the ground after a strike. Tents and convertible automobiles are not good, either. Sheltering in hard-roofed automobiles or large buildings is best, although they are rarely available to the hiker. Avoid tall structures, such as ski lifts, flagpoles, powerline towers, and the tallest trees, solitary rocks, or open hilltops. If you cannot enter a building or car, take shelter in a stand of smaller trees or in the forest. Avoid clearings. If caught in the open, crouch down on your pack or pad, or roll into a ball. If you are in water, get out. Disperse groups, so that not everyone is struck by a single bolt. Do not hold a potential lightning rod, such as a fishing pole or metal hiking pole.

Dehydration - Dry, hot summers are common along the Trail, particularly in the Virginias and the mid-Atlantic. Water may be scarce on humid days, sweat does not evaporate well, and many hikers face the danger of heat stroke and heat exhaustion if they haven't taken proper precautions, the best measures against heat emergencies are wearing a hat and sunscreen, staying well hydrated as you walk, and drinking plenty of water in camp. The following are the most common types of heat problems:

- Sunburn occurs rapidly and can be quite severe at higher elevations; hikers in the Virginias and southern Appalachians are often surprised by bad sunburn in spring, when no leaves are on the trees.

- Heat cramps are usually caused by strenuous activity in high heat and humidity, when sweating depletes salt levels in blood and tissues.

- Heat exhaustion occurs when the body's heat-regulating system breaks down. A victim may have heat cramps, sweat heavily, have cold, moist skin, and a face that is flushed, then pale.

- Heat stroke is life-threatening and occurs when the body's system of sweating fails

TEMPERATURE (°F)

Wind (mph)	40	35	30	25	20	15	10	5	0	-5	-10	-15	-20	-25	-30	-35	-40	-45
5	36	31	25	19	13	7	1	-5	-11	-16	-22	-28	-34	-40	-46	-52	-57	-63
10	34	27	21	15	9	3	-4	-10	-16	-22	-28	-35	-41	-47	-53	-59	-66	-72
15	32	25	19	13	6	0	-7	-13	-19	-26	-32	-39	-45	-51	-58	-64	-71	-77
20	30	24	17	11	4	-2	-9	-15	-22	-29	-35	-42	-48	-55	-61	-68	-74	-81
25	29	23	16	9	3	-4	-11	-17	-24	-31	-37	-44	-51	-58	-64	-71	-78	-84
30	28	22	15	8	1	-5	-12	-19	-26	-33	-39	-46	-53	-60	-67	-73	-80	-87
35	28	21	14	7	0	-7	-14	-21	-27	-34	-41	-48	-55	-62	-69	-76	-82	-89
40	27	20	13	6	-1	-8	-15	-22	-29	-36	-43	-50	-57	-64	-71	-78	-84	-91
45	26	19	12	5	-2	-9	-16	-23	-30	-37	-44	-51	-58	-65	-72	-79	-86	-93
50	26	19	12	4	-3	-10	-17	-24	-31	-38	-45	-52	-60	-67	-74	-81	-88	-95
55	25	18	11	4	-3	-11	-18	-25	-32	-39	-46	-54	-61	-68	-75	-82	-89	-97
60	25	17	10	3	-4	-11	-19	-26	-33	-40	-48	-55	-62	-69	-76	-84	-91	-98

30 min.   10 min.   5 minutes

FROSTBITE TIMES

Wind Chill (°F) = 35.74 + 0.6215T - 35.75(V$^{0.16}$) + 0.4275T(V$^{0.16}$)
Where, T= Air Temperature (°F) V= Wind Speed (mph)
National Weather Service and National Oceanic and Atmospheric Administration
Effective 11/01/01

Wind Chill Chart

Is crime a problem?

The Appalachian Trail is safer than most places, but a few crimes of violence have occurred. Awareness is one of your best lines of defense. Be aware of what you are doing, where you are, and to whom you are talking. Hikers looking out for each other can be an effective "community watch." Be prudent and cautious without allowing common sense to slip into paranoia. Remember to trust your gut—it's usually right. Other tips include the following:

- Don't hike alone. If you are by yourself and encounter a stranger who makes you feel uncomfortable, say you are with a group that is behind you. Be creative. If in doubt, move on. Even a partner is no guarantee of safety, however; pay attention to your instincts about other people.

- Leave your hiking itinerary and timetable with someone at home. Be sure your contacts and your family know your "Trail name," if you use one of those fanciful aliases common on the A.T. Check in regularly, and establish a procedure to follow if you fail to check in. On short hikes, provide your contacts with the numbers of the land-managing agencies for the area of your hike. On extended hikes, provide ATC's number, (304) 535-6331.

- Be wary of strangers. Be friendly, but cautious. Don't tell strangers your plans. Avoid people who act suspiciously, seem hostile, or are intoxicated.

- Don't camp near roads.

- Dress conservatively to avoid unwanted attention.

- Don't carry firearms. They are prohibited entirely on National Park Service lands and most other areas prohibit them without a permit. The ban on firearms remains in effect until February 22, 2010. The hiker should monitor the National Park Service website for the most current regulations prior to hiking on NPS lands. Firearms could be turned against you or result in an accidental shooting, and they are extra weight.

- Eliminate opportunities for theft. Don't bring jewelry. Hide your money. If you must leave your pack, hide it, or leave it with someone trustworthy. Don't leave valuables or equipment (especially in sight) in vehicles parked at Trailheads.

- Use the Trail registers (the notebooks stored at most shelters). Sign in using your given name, leave a note, and report any suspicious activities. If someone needs to locate you, or if a serious crime has been committed along the Trail, the first place authorities will look is in the registers.

- Report any crime or harassment to the local authorities and ATC.

Trail history

Who was Benton MacKaye, and what was his connection to the Appalachian Trail?

He first published the idea. MacKaye (1879–1973) grew up mostly in Shirley Center, Massachusetts, reading the work of American naturalists and poets and taking long walks in the mountains of Massachusetts and Vermont. MacKaye (which is pronounced like "sky") sometimes claimed that the idea for the A.T. was born one day when he was sitting in a tree atop Stratton Mountain in Vermont. But, after graduating from Harvard, he eventually went to work in the new U.S. Forest Service and began carving out a niche as a profound thinker and an advocate for wilderness. By 1919, his radical ideas had led to him being edged out of the government, and he turned his attention to creating a new discipline that later came to be called "regional planning." His initial 1921 "project in regional planning" for the A.T. was a proposal for a network of work camps and communities in the mountains, all linked by a trail that ran from the highest point in New England to the highest point in the South. He called it the Appalachian Trail.

Why did he propose it?
MacKaye was convinced that the pace of urban and industrial life along the East Coast was harmful to people. He envisioned the A.T. as a path interspersed with planned wilderness communities where people could go to renew themselves. That idea never gained much traction, but the notion of a two thousand-mile footpath in the mountains fired the imaginations of hikers and outdoorsmen from Maine to Georgia. Inspired by him, they began building trails and trying to connect them.

What was his connection to the Appalachian Trail Conference?
MacKaye was responsible for convening and organizing the first Appalachian Trail "conference" in Washington, D.C., in 1925. That gathering of hikers, foresters, and public officials embraced the goal of building the Trail. They established the Appalachian Trail Conference, appointed MacKaye as its "field organizer," and named Major William Welch, manager of New York's Harriman Park, as its first chairman.

What happened next?
Some perfunctory scouting of routes took place. A few short sections were marked and connected. New trails were built in New York. Welch designed a logo and Trail markers. Committees met in a few northeastern states and talked about the idea. But, for several years, the idea didn't really go anywhere. MacKaye was much better at inspirational abstract thinking than practical organizing, and it soon became apparent that someone else was going to have to take the lead for the Trail to actually get built.

Who pushed the project forward?
Two men, retired Judge Arthur Perkins of Connecticut and admiralty lawyer Myron Avery of Washington, D.C. Perkins took the idea and ran with it, essentially appointing himself as the

acting chairman of ATC in the late 1920s and recruiting Avery to lead the effort in the area around Washington. Both began vigorously proselytizing the idea of the Trail in 1928 and 1929, championing MacKaye's ideas to recruit volunteers, establishing hiking clubs up and down the coast, and actually going out to hike, clear brush, and mark paths themselves. As Perkins' health failed in the early 1930s, Avery took over, devoting incredible time, energy, and willpower to establishing a network of volunteers, developing clubs, working with the government, building the organization of the ATC, and setting the Trail's northern terminus at Katahdin in his native Maine. Avery remained chairman of ATC until 1952.

What was the relationship between MacKaye and Myron Avery?
They were cordial at first, but by the mid-1930s, as Avery took charge of the Trail project, they quarreled over fundamental issues and visions of what the Trail should be. Avery was more interested in hiking and in connecting the sections of the Trail, while MacKaye was more interested in the Trail's role in promoting wilderness.

When was the Trail completed?
In 1937 it fell into disrepair during World War II, when Trail maintainers were unable to work on it, and parts of the route were lost. After the war, a concerted effort was made to restore it, and it was once again declared complete in 1951.

What happened after it was completed?
It's useful to look at the Trail's history in three eras: the era of Trail-building, which lasted until the Trail was completed in 1937; the era of Trail protection, which lasted until 1968, when Congress made the A.T. a national scenic trail; and the era of management and promotion, which has lasted until the present day. The first era was dominated by personalities and focused on getting the thing built and blazed from one end to the other. The second era saw the growth of the clubs taking care of it, the growth of the Conference, the construction of shelters, and a continuing battle to keep the route open over the many hundreds of miles of private property that it crossed. The third era saw an explosion of the number of people hiking the A.T. as the government began buying land along the route to guarantee the permanence of the footpath and volunteers shifted their emphasis to the hard work of managing a part of the national park system. In July 2005, the Conference became the A.T.

Conservancy, to better state its work of protecting resources to the public.

How was the original Trail different from today's A.T.?

At first, the goal was simply to blaze a connected route. Often, this meant that the Trail led along old forest roads and other trails. Trail maintainers mostly just cleared brush and painted blazes. Today's Trail has mostly been moved off the old roads and onto new paths dug and reinforced especially for hikers. Today's route, though engineered much more elaborately, often requires more climbing, because it leads up the sides of many mountains that the old woods roads bypassed.

How do terms like "Trailway," "greenway," "buffer," and "viewshed" fit into this history?

The idea of a "Trailway" was first embraced by ATC in 1937. It meant that there was more to the Appalachian Trail than just the footpath. The "Trailway" referred to an area dedicated to the interests of those on foot, originally a mile on either side. In some cases, that came to mean a "buffer" - a legally protected area around the path that kept the sights and sounds of civilization, logging, and development away from the solitary hiker. In other cases, it meant a great deal more. It evolved into a notion of a "greenway," a broad swath of protected land through which the Trail ran. Crucial to the idea of a greenway was that of the "viewshed," the countryside visible from the Trail's high points. In the years since the A.T. became a national scenic trail, the Conservancy has worked to influence the development of surrounding areas so that the views from the Trail remain scenic, even when those views are of areas well outside the boundaries of the public Trail lands themselves.

When did Trail protection begin?

The notion of a protected zone was first formalized in an October 15, 1938, agreement between the National Park Service and the U.S. Forest Service for the promotion of an Appalachian Trailway through the relevant national parks and forests, extending one mile on each side of the Trail. Within this zone, no new parallel roads would be built or any other incompatible development allowed. Timber cutting would not be permitted within 200 feet of the Trail. Similar agreements, creating a zone one-quarter-mile in width, were signed with most states through which the Trail passes.

How were Trail lands identified?

Much of the Trail was already in national forests or national parks and state and local parks, but large portions were on private property, with the agreement of the property owners. In 1970, supplemental agreements under the 1968 National Trails Systems Act—among the National Park Service, the U.S. Forest Service, and the Appalachian Trail Conference—established the specific responsibilities of those organizations for initial mapping, selection of rights-of-way, relocations, maintenance, development, acquisition of land, and protection of a permanent Trail. Agreements also were signed between the Park Service and the various states, encouraging them to acquire and protect a right-of-way.

Why has complete protection taken so long?

Getting federal money appropriated was difficult, and not all property owners were willing to sell, which occasionally raised the specter of the government's threatening to condemn land for the Trail—always a politically unpopular action. Slow progress of federal efforts and lack of initiative by some states led Congress to strengthen the National Trails System Act in an amendment known as the Appalachian Trail Bill, which was signed by President Jimmy Carter on March 21, 1978. The new legislation emphasized the need for protecting the Trail, including acquiring a corridor, and authorized $90 million for that purpose. More money was appropriated during the Reagan, Bush, and Clinton administrations. Today, more than 99 percent of the Trail runs across public lands.

What is the relationship between the A.T. and the government, the Conservancy, and the clubs?

In 1984, the Interior Department delegated the responsibility for managing the A.T. corridor lands outside established parks and forests to the Appalachian Trail Conference. Today, the Conservancy and its Trail club partners retain primary responsibility for maintaining the footpath, too. A new, more comprehensive 10-year agreement was signed in 1994 and renewed in November 2004 for 10 years.

Trail geology

Lynn S. Fichter, Professor, Department of Geology and Environmental Science, James Madison University

Why aren't the Appalachians as high as other American mountain systems?

In a word: erosion. The modern Appalachians are not even true "mountains" in the geologic sense, but the incompletely eroded remnants of an ancient, 30,000-foot-high mountain range, the Alleghanian, that formed about 300 million years ago. In contrast, the modern Appalachians are from 3,000 to 6,000 feet high. During the continental collision that formed the Alleghanian Mountains, the ancient rocks we know as today's Appalachians were folded and faulted while deep underground.

So, what are we seeing when we look at today's Appalachians?

We see five geologic divisions (called *provinces*) that run roughly parallel to the Atlantic coast. Each province contains rocks that formed at different times in geologic history. They are, from east to west, the coastal plain, Piedmont, Blue Ridge, Ridge and Valley Province, and Allegheny Plateau.

What caused them to form?

The Appalachian rocks you see on and from the Trail are the result of the opening and closing of ocean basins. In the opening phase, a huge land mass called a supercontinent rifts into continent-sized fragments. As the continents spread apart, an ocean basin opens. The land and undersea areas along the edges of the new continent are called *divergent continental margins* (DCMs). Today's Atlantic seaboard is just such a margin, while the great valleys west of the Trail contain the remnants of an ancient DCM that formed about 500 million years ago.

What happens when an ocean basin starts to close?

When an ocean basin begins to close, and continents converge together, *subduction zones* form in the basin, where one part of the ocean floor is forced under another part, or under a continental plate, forming mountains. Such a zone under the edge of a continent builds mountains like today's Andes, at the ocean's edge. Such a zone in mid-ocean forms a *volcanic arc* of islands, like those of modern-day Japan. As the ocean basin continues to close, eventually the volcanic arc collides with a continent, building more mountains. Finally, mountains build when the ocean basin closes completely and two continental plates collide, creating the next supercontinent.

What are the geologic events recorded in the Appalachians?
The Appalachian mountains give us a geological record stretching back 1.8 billion years and containing the closing half of one cycle, which built an ancient supercontinent (called "Rodinia"), then a full cycle that built a more recent supercontinent ("Pangaea"), and finally the opening half of a third cycle that has produced the modern-day Atlantic seaboard.

What was the first Appalachian mountain-building event?
The *Grenville orogeny*, one billion years ago, is the oldest of which we have a geologic record. The ocean floor was pushed under the North American continent, building Andean-sized mountains, followed by the continent-to-continent collision that created the Rodinia supercontinent. On the Trail, you spend much of your time crossing rocks formed during the Grenville orogeny (mountain-building event).

What were the other mountain-building events?
For half a billion years, eastern North America lay in the center of a supercontinent. But, about 600 million years ago, that continent rifted apart to form what geologists call the "proto-Atlantic" (or Iapitus) ocean and a divergent continental margin. The rocks left over from that are preserved today in the great valleys west of the Trail. During the closing phase of the cycle, there were three more orogenies: the *Taconic* (a volcanic arc collision), the *Acadian* (a volcanic arc/microcontinent collision), and the *Alleghanian* (when what is now Africa collided with eastern North America, closed the proto-Atlantic, and formed Pangaea). The modern Atlantic Ocean and its present-day divergent continental margin began forming 200 million years ago.

How high were the ancient mountains?
During the Grenville and Alleghanian orogenies, Andean- and Himalayan-sized mountains formed. During the smaller Taconic and Acadian orogenies, mountains formed that were the size of today's Alps or Rockies—14,000 to 15,000 feet high.

How is each of the five Appalachian provinces different?

- The *coastal plain* is the newest and youngest. There are no mountain-built structures or rocks here, just sediment brought down to the coast from inland. The A.T. never descends to the coastal plain.

- The *Piedmont* is mostly "exotic," meaning that it contains volcanic arcs and fragments of ocean floor brought to North America from other places in the world. They are severely deformed, metamorphosed, and eroded down to their deep roots. The Trail in New Hampshire and Maine is actually part of this region, although it crosses some of the Trail's highest mountains that might not appear at first to fit the definition of "piedmont" (foothills).

- The *Blue Ridge* contains the eroded roots of the Grenville mountains, which once covered the eastern part of the continent from Texas to Quebec. Long sections of the Trail follow the Blue Ridge.

- The *Ridge and Valley Province* is made of folded and faulted sedimentary rocks and contains rocks from the proto-Atlantic, as well as sediments eroded from the Taconic and Acadian mountains. The Trail in the mid-Atlantic enters this province.

- Finally, farthest west, the *Allegheny Plateau* is made of sedimentary rocks and contains virtually a complete sedimentary record of everything since the proto-Atlantic began forming.

Why does so much of the Trail follow the Blue Ridge?

The Blue Ridge acts like a backbone for the Appalachian region and thus for the Trail. Not only is it the central province, its rocks are the oldest and stand the highest, primarily because they are still gently rising. Looking east into the Piedmont, we see the eroded remains of the Taconic and Acadian mountains. Looking west into the Ridge and Valley Province, we see the sediments eroded from those mountains that were deposited in deep basins existing there at the time. All this must be in the geological imagination, of course; none of what we see today resembles the ancient landscapes in topography, vegetation, or climate.

Why are there so many long, folded ridges today?

The modern landscape is largely the result of the Alleghenian orogeny, which folded and faulted all the previous rocks and shuffled them like a deck of cards. Virtually no rocks exposed today are where they originally formed, except for the Allegheny Plateau, west of the

A.T. During the Alleghanian orogeny, Africa rode up over the edge of North America, peeled the rocks off in layers thousands of feet thick and shoved them dozens of miles inland from their original locations. The faults and folds all run parallel to each other, and, where they bring soft rocks to the surface, erosion is easy and valleys form. The ridges are made of more erosion-resistant rocks.

What rocks are those divisions made of?

In places in Virginia, core rocks are overlain by 600-million-year-old basalt lava flows (dark green) ejected when the proto-Atlantic ocean opened. In the Smokies, many of the rocks began as sedimentary rocks of about the same age as the lava flows, moved westward from the Piedmont regions during the Alleghanian orogeny, and metamorphosed by heat and pressure. East of the Blue Ridge, and in northern New England, the rocks are all igneous and metamorphic. They include lava flows associated with several ancient volcanic arcs or rocks deposited on the sides of the volcanic arcs. Looking west from the Blue Ridge, the rocks are all sedimentary. The Roanoke Valley, Shenandoah/Page valleys, and the Great Valley of Maryland and Pennsylvania, for example, are underlain largely by limestones of the proto-Atlantic continental margin. The far mountain ridges west of the Shenandoah and Great Valley are mostly sandstones and shales from the Taconic and Acadian orogenies. All of those rocks are *thrust faulted;* that is, they consist of a series of "sheets"—a mile or more thick - that have been shoved over each other and stacked.

Were the Appalachians affected by the Ice Age?

Repeatedly. The Trail's lowest point is just southwest of where it crosses the Hudson River, a scant 124 feet above sea level. Ice Age glaciers carved the Hudson River Valley, the only fjord on the Trail. From the Delaware Water Gap north, you enter glacial country from the Ice Age that ended about 20,000 years ago, and, the farther north you go, the more glacial evidence you can see. New England mountains are typically scraped nearly bare on top, with swampy, fertile valleys where soil was deposited when the ice melted. Large *erratics,* boulders that the glaciers carried miles from the rock formations they were broken away from, appear regularly in this region. *Cirques* carved by growing glaciers, rubble hills (*terminal moraines*) formed where glaciers stopped advancing, and long, gravely mounds (*eskers*) formed by deposits from melting ice are other features. The Trail runs along some rocky ridges where the scratches and scrapes of moving ice are still visible.

Wildlife along the A.T.

How "wild" is the A.T.?

The well-known plaque at Springer Mountain in Georgia describes the A.T. as "a footpath for those who seek fellowship with the wilderness." What does that mean? The Trail will indeed take you deep into some of the wildest and most remote woodlands of the eastern United States. But, true "wilderness," in the sense of untouched wild country, is rare, even on the A.T. Much of the land that the Trail follows was once farmland—even the steep, stony, remote slopes—and nearly all of it has been logged at some time during the last four centuries. Except for bears, bobcats, and coyotes, most large natural predators have been exterminated.

In the twentieth century, though, much of the formerly settled land was incorporated into state and national parks and forests. On that land, forests and wildlife have returned. As you walk through what seems like primeval wilderness, you're likely to run across old stonewalls or abandoned logging roads or the foundations of nineteenth-century homesteads. The federal government has designated some of those areas as protected wilderness areas, which strictly limits the ways in which they can be used. Today, the mountains teem with creatures of all sorts, from microbes to moose. To the casual hiker who knows only the woods of a suburban park, it can seem very wild indeed.

One good way to look at the "wilderness" of the A.T. is as a series of long, skinny islands of wildness, surrounded by a sea of populated valleys inhabited by working farms and suburban communities. In the vast national forests of the South and the spreading timberlands of northern New England, those "islands" are somewhat broader. But, even in its wildest places, the A.T. hiker is rarely more than a strenuous day's walk from the nearest highway or community.

What large animals might I see?

Moose, the largest animal that hikers encounter along the Trail (often weighing in at more than 1,000 pounds), inhabit deep woodlands and wetlands from Massachusetts north, especially in New Hampshire and Maine. White-tailed deer can be found along the entire length of the Trail. Elk have been reintroduced to Pennsylvania, North Carolina, and Tennessee. Black bears have been spotted in all Trail states and are especially common in Georgia, North Carolina, Tennessee, Virginia, Pennsylvania, and New Jersey. Wild boars live in the Great Smoky Mountains National Park. Bobcats and coyotes are stealthy residents along most of the route of the Trail, though they're rarely seen. Fishers, otters, and beavers are occasionally reported by hikers.

What small animals might I see?
By far the most familiar will be mice, chipmunks, rabbits, and squirrels, but foxes, raccoons, opossums, skunks, groundhogs, porcupines, bats, weasels, shrews, minks, and muskrats are also common. Tree frogs and bullfrogs inhabit wet areas in warm weather, lizards scurry along rocks and fallen logs, snakes (both poisonous and nonpoisonous) are common south of New England, and streams and ponds are home to salamanders, bass, trout, bream, sunfish, and crayfish.

Which animals are dangerous?
Few A.T. hikers encounter aggressive animals, but any wild animal will fight if cornered or handled roughly—even timid animals such as deer can be quite dangerous in those circumstances. The large wild animals most likely to be aggressive include moose (during rutting season) and black bears (especially mother bears with cubs). Mountain lions, which have stalked people in western states, have long been rumored to have returned to the Appalachians, but so far scientists have not been able to confirm any sightings in mountains that the A.T. traverses.

When disturbed or stepped on, many other creatures will strike back aggressively, inflicting painful wounds or poisonous stings. Those include timber rattlesnakes and copperheads, hornets, wasps, yellow jackets, Africanized bees, and black widow and brown recluse spiders. Foxes, bats, raccoons, and other small animals susceptible to rabies may bite when suffering from infection. Mice, though not aggressive, may transmit diseases, and biting insects such as mosquitoes and ticks can infect hikers with bacteria. Hikers in more populated sections of the Trail also might encounter aggressive dogs.

What rare or endangered animal species might I see?
Birders might spot rare species such as the Bicknell's thrush, hermit thrush, gray-cheeked thrush, northern raven, olive-sided flycatcher, black-billed cuckoo, spruce grouse, bay-breasted warbler, cerulean

warbler, blackburnian warbler, magnolia warbler, blackpoll warbler, alder flycatcher, rusty blackbird, Swainson's warbler, yellow-bellied sapsucker, winter wren, red-breasted nuthatch, sharp-shinned hawk, northern saw-whet owl, golden eagle, peregrine falcon, merlin, bald eagle, and Cooper's hawk.

Harder to find, but also present, are the Carolina northern flying squirrel, Virginia northern flying squirrel, rock vole, Allegheny wood rat, eastern wood rat, water shrew, and fence lizard. The black bear and eastern timber rattlesnake, although not uncommon along the Trail, are on the rare-species list. You may also find a number of rare crustaceans, reptiles, and amphibians, including the zig-zag salamander, northern cricket frog, triangle floater mussel, Jefferson salamander, Appalachian brook crayfish, wood turtle, broadhead skink, pigmy salamander, shovelnose salamander, Shenandoah salamander, Weller's salmander, and squawfoot mussel.

What birds will I see in the Appalachians that I might not see at my backyard feeder?
Birds with summer ranges normally far to the north of where most A.T. hikers live are often found in the mountains, where the altitude makes the climate resemble that of Canada. Insect-eating birds such as whippoorwills, flycatchers, and swallows rarely show up in backyards but are common along the Trail. The songs of deep-woods birds such as the ovenbird, kinglet, veery, pewee, and red-eyed-vireo will provide an ongoing chorus for summer hikers. Pileated woodpeckers hammer deliberately on dead trees. Large game birds, such as wild turkey, ruffed grouse, and spruce grouse, forage on the forest floor and surprise hikers as they burst into flight. Many hikers linger to admire the soaring acrobatics of ravens, vultures, hawks, eagles, and falcons on the thermals and updrafts along the rocky crests of the mountains.

Trees and wild plants along the A.T.

How old are the Appalachian forests?
The forests of the Appalachians have been logged heavily for three centuries. Photographs from the late nineteenth and early twentieth centuries show many areas almost completely stripped of trees. Many Trail areas were open farmland or pastureland in the 1700s and early 1800s. Lumber is still harvested in national forests and privately owned timberlands along the Trail. Although today's mountains are

heavily forested again, it is mostly "second-growth" timber, except in a few isolated coves of "old-growth" forest that date back to precolonial times.

Forest that has grown back from burning or clearing through successive stages to the point at which it reaches a fairly steady state, with dominant full-grown trees, is known as a "climax forest." Several different climax forests appear along the A.T., and they are not mutually exclusive—different types can be found on the same mountain. The kind you encounter will depend on where you are, on what type of soil is underfoot, and the climate. The climate often depends on how high the mountains are—the higher they are, the more "northern" (or boreal) the climate.

What kinds of forests will I encounter along the Trail?

- The *mixed deciduous forest* (also called the *Southern hardwood forest)* dominates the foothills of the southern mountains and Trail lands south of New England. Various kinds of broad-leafed trees are dominant, and the understory of small trees and shrubs is profuse. Oak and hickory are the most common large trees, with maple and beech evident in more northerly sections; some sproutings of chestnut (a species that predominated until a blight devastated it early in the twentieth century) can be found as well. Understory trees such as redbud, dogwood, striped maple, and American holly are common, as are shrubs such as witch hazel, pawpaw, and mountain pepperbush.

- The *southern Appalachian forest,* found above the foothills from Georgia to central Virginia, contains more tree species than any other forest in North America and actually takes in a range of different forest types that can vary dramatically according to elevation. Climax hardwood forests of basswood, birch, maple, beech, tuliptree, ash, and magnolia can be found in some coves, while, above about 4,000 feet, the climax forests are typically spruce, fir, and hemlock, particularly on the wetter western slopes. Old-growth forest can be found in isolated parts of the Great Smoky Mountains National Park. Oak forests often predominate on the eastern faces of the mountains, which typically do not receive as much moisture. Pine and oak may mix on some slopes. At higher elevations, the understory is less varied: Shrubs of mountain laurel and rhododendron form nearly impenetrable thickets that are densest where conditions are wettest.

- The *transition forest* tends to be wetter and more northerly than the mixed deciduous forest. Hikers marveling at the colors of a New England fall are admiring the transition forest. It extends across the hillsides and lowlands of the north and reaches down into the high country of the southern Appalachians. It appears as a mosaic of spruce, fir, hemlock, pine, birch, maple, basswood, and beech forests. The substory of transition forest tends to be more open, with ferns and shrubs of elderberry, hazel, and bush honeysuckle, and often a thick carpet of evergreen needles covers the ground under the trees. Conifers tend to predominate at the higher elevations.

- The northern, or *boreal forest,* is the largest North American forest. Most of it is in Canada and Alaska, but A.T. hikers encounter it while traversing the highest ridges of the southern Appalachians and the coniferous uplands of northern New England. Pines and hemlocks characterize its southern reaches, while dwarfed spruces and firs (known as *krummholz* or *taiga*) grow at treeline in New Hampshire and Maine, just as they grow at the borders of the arctic lands farther north. In between is a spruce-fir climax forest. Evergreens such as white pine, red pine, white spruce, balsam fir, black spruce, and jack pine predominate, but hardwoods such as aspen and birch are mixed in as well. The ground of the boreal forest is typically thin and muddy, with little in the way of an understory, and it includes sphagnum bogs surrounded by a wide variety of aquatic plants, ferns, subalpine plants, blueberry bushes, and mountain maple and ash shrubs.

What wildflowers can I look for, and when will I see them?

Among the small joys of hiking the Trail are the wildflowers that grow along the way. Some poke their heads out of the forest duff in late winter and are gone by the time the spreading canopy of late-spring trees blocks out the sun. Some cluster near the edges of clearings in midsummer, while others hide in the deep shade. And, still others blossom amid the falling leaves and early snows of the Appalachian fall.

Winter/early spring - First to bloom in swampy areas most years is the maroon-colored cowl that shelters the tiny, foul-smelling flowers of skunk cabbage, which may appear while snow is still on the ground. In March and April, along the high, dry ridges, the delicate starbursts of bloodroot appear, along with the corncob-like clusters of squaw root on fallen oak trees; the graceful, lily-like dogtooth violet; the white bunches of early saxifrage; fanlike, purple clusters of dwarf iris in southern sections, the pink-purple flowers and liver-shaped leaves of hepatica; the delicate, white rue anemone; the bee-buzzing carpets of fringed phacelia in the South; and the waxy, pink trailing arbutus farther north.

Spring/early summer - During May and June, as the tree canopy shades the forest floor, the variety of wildflowers blooming along the A.T. becomes too extensive to keep track of. The bubblegum scent and orange blooms of flame azalea shrubs burst out in the southern Appalachians, along with the white and pink blossoms of its close relatives, mountain laurel and rhododendron. The garlicky wild leek, or ramp, flowers in early summer. Hikers may spot the green tubes of jack-in-the-pulpit, dove-like red clusters of wild columbine, vessel-like orchid blossoms of pink lady's-slipper, spade-leaved trillium, bright blue of viper's bugloss, the blue-violet of spiderwort in sunny clearings, black cohosh's delicate cone of tiny blooms, and, in the cold bogs of the northern states, the white blossoms of Labrador tea and the pink pentagons of bog laurel.

Late summer - The heat of July and August in the Appalachians coaxes blossoms from a number of mountain shrubs, shade plants, and meadow plants. The wintergreen shrub blooms white in oak forests, the white starbursts of tall meadow rue appear near open fields, the white petals of the bug-trapping sundew appear in wet areas, mountain cranberry's small bell-like pink blossoms appear in New England, the white-and-yellow sunbursts of oxeye daisy grow along hedgerows, and the greenish-white clusters of wild sarsaparilla appear in the dry, open woods. In the mid-Atlantic states, the understory becomes a waist-deep sea of wood nettle, the delicate white flowers of which belie unpleasant stinging hairs that bristle from the stems and leaves; the succulent stalks of jewel-weed, which has a pale yellow flower, often sprout nearby, and their juice can help ease the sting and itch of the nettles and poison ivy.

Fall and early winter - Certain wildflowers continue blooming late into the fall along the A.T., disappearing from the woods about the same time hikers do. Goldenrod spreads across open fields in September, about the time the leaves start changing color. The intricate white discs of Queen Anne's lace adorn ditches and roadsides until late in the year. Other common fall wildflowers include aster, wood sorrel, monkshood, and butter-and-eggs.

Can I eat wild plants I find?

You could eat certain plants, but, in keeping with the principles of Leave No Trace, you probably shouldn't. Leave the wild blueberries and raspberries and blackberries of summer for the birds and bears. Resist the temptation to spice up your noodles with ramps in the spring. "Chicken of the woods" mushrooms should stay in the woods. Wild watercress belongs in a stream, not a salad. Rather than brewing your own ginseng or sassafras tea from wild roots, visit the supermarket in town. Many edible plants along the A.T. are rare and endangered, and harvesting them is illegal. Even when the flora are plentiful, remember that the fauna of the Appalachians have no option other than to forage for it; you do.

What rare or endangered plant species might I see?

Most of the federally listed plant species (threatened or endangered) along the Appalachian Trail are found in the high country of the southern Appalachians or the alpine environments of northern New England. There are too many to list here, but typical of those in the southern Appalachians is the spreading avens, a plant with fan-shaped leaves and small, yellow flowers that grows in rock crevices. Although bluets are common along the A.T., a subspecies called Roan Mountain bluet is found in only nine sites there—the only known sites in the world. Gray's lily is found only on the high balds near Roan Mountain. Although goldenrod is plentiful along the Trail and sometimes considered something of a pest, one rare subspecies, the Blue Ridge goldenrod, is known to exist only on one cliff in North Carolina. Similarly, many of the plants at and above treeline in New England, such as Robbins cinquefoil, are extremely vulnerable to damage from hikers wandering off the A.T. Below treeline, plants such as the small whorled pogonia, an orchid, are threatened by development. Please don't pick the flowers along the A.T.—they might be the only ones of a kind.

The how and why of Trail construction

Who decides which route the Trail takes?

A local Trail-maintaining club, in consultation with the Appalachian Trail Conservancy and the government agency responsible for managing the land in question, determines the route that the footpath follows over a section. According to the National Trails System Act that authorized federal protection of the A.T., the goal is to expose the walker to "the maximum outdoor recreation potential and enjoyment of the nationally significant scenic, historic, natural, or cultural qualities of the area." In plain language, that means routing the Trail in such a way that walkers have the chance to encounter and appreciate the wildlife, geography, and geology, as well as the historical and natural context of the Appalachians, while merging with, exploring, and harmonizing with the mountain environment.

How is today's A.T. different from the original Trail?

When the A.T. was first built, the main goal was a continuous, marked route, which often meant connecting existing footpaths and woods roads. Long sections of "roadwalks" linked the footpaths. Where no existing routes were available, Trail builders marked out new ones, cleared brush, and painted blazes. But, that was about it, and, for many years, when few people knew about or hiked the Trail, it was enough. Beginning in the 1960s, though, two things happened: The A.T. became a part of the national park system, and the numbers of people using it began skyrocketing. With increased use, mud and erosion became problems. As the Trail was moved away from existing footpaths and roads and onto new paths planned and built especially for the A.T. on federal land, Trail builders began "hardening" the path and designing it to stand up to heavier use.

What causes the Trail to deteriorate?

Water is the main culprit. Erosion can damage the footpath quickly. The mineral soil of the footpath is made of very fine particles bound together by clay that, once broken from the ground by boots and hiking poles, is easily washed away by fast-flowing water. (Water moving at two miles per hour has sixty-four times more ability to carry soil particles than water moving at one mile per hour.) Today's Trail builders work to separate water from the treadway. Where that is not possible, they try to slow it down. Since water in rivulets or ruts flows faster than water flowing across the Trail in sheets, trail builders try to channel water off the part that hikers walk on. Where they can't, they slant the path outward so that water will stay "thin" and flow slowly off the sides in a sheet, rather than becoming "thick" and channeling down the middle of the Trail.

Trail builders work to separate water from the treadway by constructing the trail at grades gentle enough and with sufficient outward slope to the tread to allow water to run across it rather than be captured by it and run down the trail. When that is not possible, they try to slow it down or divert it off the trail as quickly as possible.

Why are parts of the Trail routed over narrow log walkways?

Believe it or not, it's not to keep your feet dry. The goal is to protect the land, not your nice, new boots. Bog bridges, also called "puncheon," allow the Trail to take hikers into an important part of the mountain environment without turning such ecologically sensitive swamp areas into hopeless quagmires, disrupting plant and animal life there. The Trail is supposed to "wear lightly on the land," and this is one way to do so. Walkways may be built on piles driven into the ground, or they may "float" on boggy ground; in both cases, the wetlands are disturbed much less than they would be by mud holes that widen every time a hiker tries to skirt the edges.

Why does the Trail zigzag up steep mountains?

When it was first marked, the Trail often climbed steep slopes by the most direct route, and older parts of today's Trail still tend to have the steepest sections. But, water runs faster down a steeper trail and erodes it more quickly. In recent years, many sections have been rerouted so that the Trail ascends by way of "sidehill" that slants up a mountainside and "switchbacks" that zigzag across its steepest faces. Again, it isn't done to make the Trail easier for hikers, although that's sometimes the effect, but rather to make the footpath itself more durable and less subject to erosion.

How does the Trail cross creeks and rivers?

Bridges take the Trail across all its major river crossings, except for the Kennebec River in Maine (where hikers ferry across in canoes). Most, such as the Bear Mountain Bridge across the Hudson in New York, are highway bridges; a few others, such as the James River Foot Bridge in Virginia, are built especially for foot travelers. A few large creeks require fording, but most are crossed by footbridges or stepping stones. Small streams may require fording when spring floods submerge the rocks and stepping stones that lead across them.

Why are there so many logs and rock barriers in the path?
Unless the logs result from a "blowdown" (a fallen tree) or the rocks from a rockslide, they're probably water-diversion devices, such as waterbars or check dams that have been added to older, eroding sections of the Trail. Avoid stepping on them, if possible: Not only can they be slippery (particularly the logs), but they will last longer if you step over them.

Why is the Trail so rocky?
As you may have read in the section of this guide devoted to geology, the Appalachians are the product of erosion, which tends to strip away soil and leave rocks on the surface. Since rocky sections offer a durable surface and often provide spectacular views for hikers, Trail designers don't hesitate to route the footpath along them. This is particularly true from central Virginia through Connecticut and eastern New Hampshire through Maine; many older sections of the Trail are routed along ridgelines. Typically, the A.T. will climb a ridge on smoother "sidehill" Trail and then follow a rocky ridgeline for some distance, before descending again.

THE TRAIL ROUTE IN PENNSYLVANIA

From the Delaware Water Gap and the Borough of Delaware Water Gap the Trail climbs over 1,100 feet, with views of the river below, before reaching Mt. Minsi. From here the Trail follows the flat ridge crest with slight dips into Totts Gap and Fox Gap. After passing over Wolf Rocks the Trail descends into Wind Gap. The whole northern section of the Trail in Pennsylvania has springs that are unreliable after early summer.

After climbing out of Wind Gap, the Trail stays on the ridge, crossing Smith Gap, dipping into and climbing out of Little Gap, and then passing over an open rocky area before dropping sharply into Lehigh Gap to cross the Lehigh River. The Trail climbs out of Lehigh Gap and stays on the ridge for nearly 30 miles before dropping down the side and passing near the Hawk Mountain Sanctuary at Eckville. A gradual climb then leads to the Pinnacle, considered by many people to be the most spectacular viewpoint along the Trail in Pennsylvania.

The Trail next drops into Windsor Furnace before regaining the ridge, and then dropping steeply to the Schuykill River at the town of Port Clinton. A steep 1,000-foot climb leads to 30 more miles of ridge top hiking until the descent into Swatara Gap. Here the Trail leaves Blue Mountain and traverses St. Anthony's Wilderness. crossing Second Mountain, Sharp Mountain, Stony Mountain, and finally ascending Peters Mountain which it follows for about 15 miles before dropping steeply to the Susquehanna River and the town of Duncannon.

Beyond the Susquehanna, the Trail turns southwest, crossing Cove Mountain and Blue Mountain before entering the great twelve-mile wide Cumberland Valley. Through here the Trail has been relocated to an off-road route thanks to land acquisitions by the National Park Service. Here the trail passes along a narrow corridor of NPS land through rich Pennsylvania agricultural lands and suburbia. At the southern edge of the valley the Trail climbs South Mountain and enters Michaux State Forest, passing through Pine Grove Furnace and Caledonia State Parks before leaving the plateau-like top of the South Mountain range and entering Maryland at Pen Mar.

HISTORY ALONG THE TRAIL

PRE-HISTORY AND HISTORY OF THE REGION

Topography - It is the arc of mountains extending from northeast to southwest in Pennsylvania that is essentially followed by the Appalachian Trail in its passage through the state. With some justification it has been argued that of all the natural features in the Keystone State none has influenced the course of history more than its mountains; and of those mountains, none carries more of history's mark than the ridges on which the A.T. finds itself. Not surprisingly therefore, the ebb and flow of historic events have left their traces in many places along the Trail's route. These signs are sometimes obvious, sometimes subtle and discernible only with some effort. Awareness of the impact of history on the region traversed by the A.T., however, can serve to enhance any hiking experience.

Native Americans - Hikers interested in Native American history along the Trail often speculate on the identity of the particular tribe that inhabited the region. Such thinking, alas, goes instantly to the heart of much misunderstanding of the nature of Indian culture. Indians tended to move about considerably and the names by which they were known reflected their language or bloodlines rather than some particular area. Nevertheless, at the time of the arrival of the first European settlers, the Delaware River Valley generally was occupied by the Lenni-Lenape, who spoke one of the Algonquian languages. It was the English settlers who assigned to them the name by which they are generally known: Delawares. By the late 1600s, however, this entire region was controlled by the Iroquois. Along with the Iroquois, the Delawares enjoyed a culture that had highly developed concepts of government, education, and morality. Although it lacked the intricate theological superstructure of the religions of the European settlers, the Delawares also had a finely developed religion.

The interaction between the Indian and European cultures is now known to have been much greater than is commonly realized. Indians provided the Europeans with their first introductions to such agricultural products as potatoes, corn, beans, squash, and tomatoes.

With less happy long-term results, they also introduced the new settlers to the joys of tobacco. The network of well-defined Indian paths (of which the Appalachian Trail, except for rare stretches, was not one) provided access to much of the interior of the province. The Indian languages also live on in a variety of ways, but mostly through a host of place names, not only in Pennsylvania but also throughout most of the U.S.

EARLY INDUSTRY

Charcoal Iron - Of the early industries that have left a mark on the land still discernible to the passing Appalachian Trail hiker, three stand out: iron manufacturing, coal mining, and the railroads.

From 1740 until after the Civil War the charcoal iron industry flourished in Pennsylvania. At its peak in about 1840 the charcoal iron industry employed more than 11,000 workers at 113 furnaces and 169 bloomeries, forges and rolling mills. (A bloomery is a special hearth for smelting iron into shapes suitable for the production of wrought iron.) In many parts of southeastern and central Pennsylvania were found high quality iron ores much sought after by gun and tool makers. Nearby was generally an abundance of forest to provide the wood from which was produced the charcoal used to fuel the iron furnaces. The combination of these resources resulted in a thriving industry that lasted until the arrival of coal as an iron-making fuel made the proximity of forests irrelevant.

Railroads - In the early 1800s, the railroad began to supplant the canals in Pennsylvania as the principal means of transporting goods and people. At the start of the Civil War, Pennsylvania had just less than 2,600 miles of railroad track. By 1900, this mileage had grown to over 10,000. In many places, long stretches of former railroad bed have been turned into hiking paths. A number of these are encountered along the route of the A.T. in Pennsylvania.

Coal Mining - St Anthony's Wilderness is an area where some marginal coal seams were mined in the last century. The coal here was thin and quickly exhausted, leaving behind some traces of a long-gone culture.

HISTORY OBSERVED FROM THE TRAIL

Franklin's Forts - Although the hiker will look in vain for any physical remains of Franklin's French and Indian War forts, there are markers here and there. Just west of PA Rt. 183, along the Appalachian Trail, is a historical marker for Fort Dietrich Snyder, which was supposedly a lookout post for Fort Northkill.

St. Anthony's Wilderness - Between Pa. Rt. 443 and Pa. Rt. 325, the Appalachian Trail passes through a magnificent stretch of wilderness unbroken by habitation for 14 miles. This land is now owned and managed by the Pennsylvania Game Commission. See Section 7 for more history of this area.

Iron Industry and Furnaces East of the Susquehanna - At many places along the Appalachian Trail in Pennsylvania the hiker is likely to encounter flat round areas, between 30 and 50 feet in diameter. These are charcoal hearths where wood was burned to produce charcoal, which was used to fuel the iron furnaces that flourished from 1740 until after the Civil War.

Two miles down from the Trail on the Lehigh Furnace Gap Road are the ruins of the Lehigh Iron Furnace, built in 1826. The remains are 30 feet high and in fairly good condition.

Directly along the Trail, between Eckville and Port Clinton, is the site of the former Windsor Furnace. Nothing remains of this structure, although some glassy slag can still be found in the footpath.

Pine Grove Furnace - The basis of the iron and steel industry was the charcoal-fired blast furnace and forge of pre-Revolutionary times. In 1762 there was a furnace, owned by the Ege family, which is still standing at Boiling Springs, and one at Pine Grove, where firearms were made for the Revolution. By 1850 there were ten ironworks in the South Mountain area, most of which were on the Cumberland Valley side, but three were located near the present route of the A.T. See Section 12 for more history of this area.

Caledonia Iron Works - The ruins of the Caledonia Iron Works furnace, which was built in 1837, can be seen in the parking lot at the corner of U.S. Rt. 30 and Pa. Rt. 233 in Caledonia State Park.

Thaddeus Stevens, the famous abolitionist, owned these works at the time of the Civil War. See Section 13 for more history of this area.

Pen Mar Park - On the southern border of Pennsylvania, the Appalachian Trail runs through the old Pen Mar Park. See Section 14 for more history of this area.

Acknowledgment is made of extensive reliance on "A History of Pennsylvania" by Philip S. Klein and Ari Hoogenboom; Published by McGraw-Hill, Inc.; 1973.

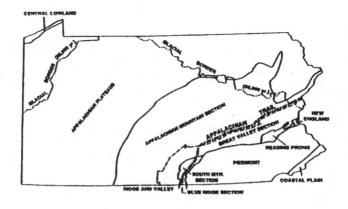

GEOLOGY ALONG THE TRAIL

Introduction - The Appalachian Trail passes through two physiographic provinces between the Delaware Water Gap and Pen Mar.

1-a. Appalachian Mountain section of the Ridge and Valley province;
1-b. Great Valley section of the Ridge and Valley province
2.   South Mountain section of the Blue Ridge province.

Each of these areas has a characteristic topography that reflects the various rock types present and the geologic history of those rocks. The three sections are described as follows:

APPALACHIAN MOUNTAIN SECTION:
Ridge and Valley Province

The A.T. follows ridgelines from the Delaware Water Gap to Pa. 944 west of the Susquehanna River. These ridges are broken periodically by wind gaps and water gaps. Formed by erosion-resistant quartzites and conglomerates, the ridges are strewn with frost-weathered rock debris, seen as felsenmeer and boulderfields. The mountains rise about 1,000 feet above adjacent valleys which are underlain by more easily eroded shale, siltstone, and limestone.

Bedrock in these mountains ranges in age from 440 to 320 million years; it is sandstone, quartzite, siltstone, conglomerate, shale, and a little coal. All of these rock units were deformed by mountain building activity which culminated about 270 million years ago, and changed the original horizontal attitude of the rocks into that of steeply dipping, near vertical, or overturned beds. Millions of years of subsequent erosion have produced the landscape present today.

About 20,000 years ago a continental glacier extended south into Pennsylvania intercepting the area of the Trail in a small section near Delaware Water Gap. Two older continental glaciations which had occurred, about 150,000 years ago and more than 700,000 years ago occupied the valleys on either side of the ridge in the Delaware Water Gap area, but there is no evidence that any of these glacial advances had covered the ridge.

During these glacial periods, climatic conditions in Pennsylvania beyond the ice border were severe and probably had permafrost to some depth. Repetitive freeze-thaw cycles occurred everywhere, particularly on south-facing slopes at higher elevations. These cycles subjected the ridge-crest rocks to ice wedging in open, water-saturated fractures. Rock fragments from ridge-crest outcrops accumulated as large masses of talus, or scree. Broken, angular rock fragments and weathered outcrops common along the ridge crest are a product of this periglacial climate-induced, physical breakup of the bedrock.

GREAT VALLEY SECTION:
Ridge and Valley Province

This division extends from Pa. Rt. 944 at the foot of Blue Mountain 13.8 miles to Yellow Breeches Creek at the foot of South Mountain. The topography is characterized by a broad, open undulating valley, part of the Great Valley section extending from central New York through Virginia into Tennessee. The Trail crosses this valley at one of its narrow points (approximately 12 miles) reaching South Mountain.

This valley is underlain by intensely deformed limestone, dolomite and shale with narrow, cross-cutting diabase dikes, locally called "ironstone". Most bedrock in the valley ranges in age from 560 to 440 million years, while the diabase is approximately 180 million years old. All the rock units except the diabase weather readily in the humid Northeast climate. The diabase is more resistant to erosion than the adjacent rocks, standing as a narrow ridge across part of the valley. The Appalachian Trail follows part of this "Iron-Stone Ridge."

SOUTH MOUNTAIN SECTION:
Blue Ridge Province

This division extends from the Yellow Breeches 56 miles to Pen Mar and beyond. The topography is characterized by rounded, relatively gentle knobs ranging in elevation from about 550 to 1,190 feet above the valley floor. White Rocks, near the northeastern tip of the province, is an exception; there the topography is steep and rugged, and capped by a spine of hard, vitreous quartzite bedrock.

The rocks of South Mountain are the oldest encountered along the Trail in Pennsylvania, ranging in age from about 600 to 560 million years. These rocks also exhibit the most complex geologic relationships. The mountain range is a broad, composite, anticlinal (upfold) structure that has been thrust and overturned along deep-seated, regional fault zones during crustal shortening. Bedrock is composed of vitreous quartzite, phyllite, conglomeratic quartzite, graywacke and metamorphosed volcanic rocks, all of which are more resistant to erosion than rocks in adjoining valleys.

The geology of the Appalachian Trail in Pennsylvania is described in greater detail in a publication by the Pennsylvania Geological Survey entitled *The Geology of the Appalachian Trail in Pennsylvania,* (General Geology Report 74), by the late John P. (Pete) Wilshusen, a longtime KTA member and a member of the staff of the Pennsylvania Topographic and Geologic Survey.

HAWK MOUNTAIN SANCTUARY

The Appalachian Trail passes through a corridor adjacent to the eastern boundary of one of the most famous wildlife areas in the world--Hawk Mountain Sanctuary. The Sanctuary is accessible to A.T. hikers by a blue-blazed spur trail which continues along the ridge after the A.T. drops down through the valley to the south or heads north towards PA Rt. 309.

The Sanctuary, founded in 1934, was the first refuge developed to protect birds of prey as they migrated along the ridge in the fall of the year. Prior to its establishment, Hawk Mountain was the gathering place for hundreds of gunners who would engage in the wholesale slaughter of hawks, falcons, and eagles as the birds passed by the North Lookout.

Now persons come from around the world to visit the Sanctuary year round to witness the migration of birds. From mid-August through mid-December some 18,000 birds of prey representing 16 species are recorded, sometimes at a remarkably close range, from one of several lookout points accessible by footpaths.

Since the Sanctuary is a private, non-profit educational institution, an admission fee is collected. Hikers are encouraged to use the honor system by attempting to cover the $5.00 ($7.00 on autumn weekends) admission charge, either at the Visitor Center or the trail entrance. Hawk Mountain Sanctuary celebrates its 75th anniversary in 2009.

Membership in the Hawk Mountain Sanctuary Association allows free admission to the trails as well as many other benefits. No camping, fires, or pets are allowed on Sanctuary property or along the clearly-marked Hawk Mountain/A.T. Corridor.

For further information write:

Hawk Mountain Sanctuary
1700 Hawk Mountain Rd
Kempton, PA 19529
www.hawkmountain.org

LAND OWNERSHIP

PENNSYLVANIA GAME COMMISSION

The Pennsylvania Game Commission, established in 1895, owns nearly 1.4 million acres of land in Pennsylvania. The land is managed for the propagation and preservation of wildlife. The agency is self-supporting and receives the major portion of its income from hunting and trapping license sales, timber sales, and federal aid reimbursements. The Commission is an independent administrative state agency providing Commonwealth citizens with the opportunity both to hunt and to enjoy wildlife on a nonconsumptive basis. The Game Commission recognizes the use of State Game Lands by non-hunters such as photographers, birders, and hikers, and encourages these activities. Financial support of the Game Commission by non-hunters is welcome. Such support can be through the purchase of a license or by participating in programs designed to benefit nongame wildlife. Funds for these programs are raised through sales of wildlife stamps, patches, and prints. Direct contributions can also be made to specific nongame programs such as "Working Together for Wildlife."

The Game Commission has extensive holdings on Blue Mountain, which is the basic route of the Appalachian Trail from west of the Susquehanna River to the Delaware Water Gap. As a result, 72 miles of Appalachian Trail in this section traverses through and is protected by the State Game Lands.

From November 15 through December 15 hikers are required to wear daylight fluorescent orange-colored material. Hikers may be fined for not following the rules. According to the PA Code: Except on Sundays, be present on State game lands from November 15 through December 15 inclusive when not engaged in lawful hunting or trapping and fail to wear a minimum of 250 square inches of daylight fluorescent orange-colored material on the head, chest and back combined or, in lieu thereof, a hat of the same colored material. The material shall be worn so it is visible in a 360° arc. Persons using shooting ranges are exempted from this requirement.

Camping and establishing campsites are prohibited on State Game Lands with some specific exceptions along the A.T. One exception is Rausch Gap Shelter in Game Lands #211. Here, because there is extensive mileage in both directions on the Appalachian Trail within the boundaries of the Game Lands, this shelter was authorized for the use of thru-hikers passing through St. Anthony's Wilderness. Hikers may stay at the shelter for only one night. The Game Commission also permits primitive camping along the Appalachian Trail, for long distance hikers only, as it traverses Game Lands. The rules for primitive camping by A.T. thru-hikers in State Game Lands are as follows:

1. Camp within 200 feet of the Trail
2. Camp one night only at any given site.
3. Do **NOT** camp within 500 feet of a water source or public access.
4. **NO** open fires when the fire index rating used by DCNR is high, very high, or extreme.

For more information about Pennsylvania State Game Lands, write:

Pennsylvania Game Commission
2001 Elmerton Avenue
Harrisburg, PA 17110-9797
717-787-4250
http://www.pgc.state.pa.us

PENNSYLVANIA BUREAU OF FORESTRY

Forty-five miles of the Appalachian Trail in Pennsylvania are located on State Forest lands. About 39 miles are on the Michaux State Forest, which the A.T. crosses shortly after it enters the state from the south. The remaining six miles are divided between the Weiser and Delaware State Forests.

The purpose of the State Forests, according to law, is: "To provide a continuous supply of timber, lumber, wood and other forest products, to protect the watersheds, conserve the waters, and regulate the flow of rivers and streams of the state, and to furnish opportunities for healthful recreation to the public." State Forest lands are open for the enjoyment of the public by their administrators, the Bureau of Forestry of the Department of Conservation and Natural Resources.

The most valuable resource on the Michaux State forest is water. All or part of fifteen municipal watersheds are located on the Michaux State Forest, and collectively they comprise approximately 24% of the total acreage in this forest district. As you walk the Appalachian Trail you will be in or very close to many of these watersheds.

On State Forest lands the Appalachian Trail is contained within a buffer zone where timber harvesting is restricted to the removal of hazardous trees that pose a risk to public safety.

Primitive camping is permitted along the main Trail and along most of the side trails on State Forest Land, except within one mile of an adjoining State Park. Open fires are prohibited when the forest-fire danger is determined by the District Forester to be High, Very High or Extreme and from March 1 through May 25 and from October 1 through December 1 without authorization from the District Forester or a designee. This prohibition does not apply to small self-contained camp stoves when used in a safe manner.

For information about State Forest Land, contact:

Pennsylvania Department of Conservation and Natural Resources
Bureau of Forestry
PO Box 8552
Harrisburg, PA 17105
717-783-7941
http://www.dcnr.state.pa.us

PENNSYLVANIA BUREAU OF STATE PARKS

The Appalachian Trail passes through portions of the following State Parks from south to north:

<u>Caledonia State Park</u>, 101 Pine Grove Road, Fayetteville, PA 17222-8224 (717-352-2161; caledoniasp@state.pa.us) is one of the oldest State Parks in Pennsylvania. Located in Franklin and Adams Counties midway between Chambersburg and Gettysburg, it is on U.S. Route 30. The A.T. skirts the busy day use area.

Pine Grove Furnace State Park, 1100 Pine Grove Road, Gardners, PA 17324-8837 (717-486-7174; pinegrovesp@state.pa.us) is located in the heart of Michaux State Forest in southern Cumberland County. The park took its name from the Pine Grove Iron Furnace, the remains of which still stand. The furnace dates back to 1764. Other buildings dating back to the old iron making community also still remain. The historic significance of the area was recognized in 1977 when the iron making area was entered in the National Register of Historical Places.

The first recreational facilities were built in the area by the railroad. The area was later purchased by the Commonwealth of Pennsylvania in 1913.

Two small lakes are situated within the 696-acre mountain park. The first Fuller Lake, 1.7 acres in size, was the hole from which the iron ore was mined for Pine Grove Furnace. The Fuller Lake recreation area includes facilities for swimming, picnicking, family camping, organized youth group tenting, and fishing.

The second lake is the 25-acre Laurel Lake, where picnicking, swimming, nonpower boating, and fishing facilities are available. The Appalachian Trail passes through the central portion of the park with busy day use areas. A parking area near the old iron furnace is provided for the parking of trail hikers' vehicles. Register the vehicle at the park office. A hiker's log is also kept at the camp store, which is open during the summer season and for limited hours during the rest of the year.

Located along the Appalachian Trail, as hikers enter the park from the south, the Ironmaster's Mansion is now an AYH Hostel. Overnight lodging, hot showers, cooking facilities, a game room, and a hot tub are available for hikers. Contact the hostel at 717-486-7575 for more information. The Grist Mill will be the home of the Appalachian Trail Museum

Ibberson Conservation Area, A half of a mile of the A.T. passes through a portion of the Ibberson Conservation Area. Numerous trails allows hikers to explore the conservation area. The 1.8 mile blue-blazed Victoria Trail intersects the A.T. After he graduated from Yale University in 1948, Joseph E. Ibberson went to work for the Commonwealth of Pennsylvania. He developed some of the forestry management plans for the 2,000,000 acres of state forests. Ibberson also helped to create the many divisions within what is now the Pennsylvania Department of Conservation and Natural Resources. He donated this 370 acre tract of land on December 9, 1998 to DCNR.

This became the first conservation area in the Pennsylvania Bureau of State Parks.

Swatara State Park, c/o Memorial Lake State Park, Grantville, PA 17028-9682 (717-865-6470; fax 717-865-7289; memorialsp@state.pa.us;) consists of 3,516 acres extending northeast from Swatara Gap for 7.5 miles along the Swatara Creek Valley. Currently undeveloped, the park nevertheless offers recreational opportunities for hiking, hunting, bicycling, fishing, canoeing and rafting, and ski touring. Construction is anticipated to start in 2010 or 2011. During construction be aware of potential temporary reroutes of the trail.

For general information about Pennsylvania's State Parks, contact:

Pennsylvania Department of Conservation and Natural Resources
Bureau of State Parks
P.O. Box 8767
Harrisburg, Pennsylvania 17105-8767
1-888-PA- PARKS
http://www.dcnr.state.pa.us/stateparks

PENNSYLVANIA FISH AND BOAT COMMISSION

At Boiling Springs the Trail follows the shore of Children's Lake, using a corridor that was acquired by the Trust for Appalachian Trail Lands with the help of a local benefactor and the Pennsylvania Fish and Boat Commission. Management of the lake is the responsibility of the Fish and Boat Commission.

NATIONAL PARK SERVICE

Pursuant to passage in 1968 of the National Trails System Act, which established the Appalachian Trail as one of the nation's first two National Scenic Trails, the National Park Service (NPS) has undertaken to protect those miles of the Trail that are outside existing state and federal units, and which could not be covered by state protection programs.

NPS's protection program in Pennsylvania is now nearly complete. Nearly 100 miles of the Trail in Pennsylvania will lie in a protected corridor on lands acquired by NPS. In addition to making the necessary connections between existing public lands, the Trail corridor was located to favor the highest land, minimize impacts to private landowners, and take advantage of features attractive to hikers.

In an unprecedented move, the National Park Service in 1984 conveyed to ATC management responsibility for recently acquired NPS lands outside existing federally administered areas. ATC, in turn, has assigned responsibility to its appropriate member clubs. The National Park Service retains a responsibility and an interest in seeing that these lands and their resources are managed "to provide for maximum outdoor recreation potential and for the conservation and enjoyment of the nationally significant scenic, historic, natural or cultural qualities of the areas through which such trails may pass." (Sec. 3b of the National Trails System Act)

There are no ATVs, horses, bikes, car camping, or hunting allowed on NPS land.

The National Park Service remains an active and committed partner in the cooperative management of the Appalachian Trail.

PRIVATE LAND

Although a very high percentage of the Trail in Pennsylvania is now on publicly owned land, many sections abut private property. Whether publicly or privately owned land hikers should leave no trace of passage.

•Do not destroy or damage trees.
•Do not damage fences or leave gates open.
•Do not litter the trail.
•Do not disturb crops or animals.
•Be careful of fires; build them only at designated camp sites.
•Carry out your trash. (If you carried it in, you can carry it out.)
•Take nothing but pictures; leave nothing but footprints.

GENERAL INFORMATION

TRAIL MAINTENANCE

The work of maintaining the shelters and cabins, and keeping the trails cleared and blazed is done by volunteers - over 15,000 hours per year in Pennsylvania alone! No one is paid for any trail work. Each section of the Trail is assigned to a club. You will find the name of the maintaining organization or organizations at the beginning of each Trail Description Section under General Information.

Although you are certainly encouraged to toss aside blowdowns and to clean up around shelters, you should not attempt to do any trail marking or relocating on your own. Instead, join an A.T. maintaining club and offer your services through it. For a list of the names and addresses of organizations affiliated with Keystone Trails Association see the list below. Any unusual trouble spots along the Trail should be reported to KTA or to the Appalachian Trail Conservancy Mid-Atlantic Regional Office at phone 717-258-5771 or email atc-maro@appalachiantrail.org.

RIDGERUNNER PROGRAM

While hiking the Trail you may meet a Ridgerunner, an individual hired through the Appalachian Trail Conservancy, to hike sections of the Trail. The primary goal of the Ridgerunner is to provide information and education to users of the backcountry by explaining existing rules, regulations, and low impact practices, to monitor the trail and assist local trail managers. Through the Ridgerunner program, the Trail and the environment are protected and hikers benefit from important information or assistance.

The Ridgerunner Program is financially supported by the PA Department of Conservation and Natural Resources, Appalachian Trail Conservancy, Wilmington Trail Club, BATONA Hiking Club, AMC-Delaware Valley Chapter, Philadelphia Trail Club, Mountain Club of Maryland, Susquehanna A.T. Club, Cumberland Valley Appalachian Trail Club, and the Potomac Appalachian Trail Club. BMECC utilizes a volunteer ridgerunner to cover their section.

MAINTAINING CLUBS IN PENNSYLVANIA

The accompanying diagram, "Pennsylvania Appalachian Trail Maintenance Assignments" depicts the relative maintenance responsibility of each club.

Shown below is the contact website for each of the Pennsylvania maintaining clubs. If you are unable to reach a club, contact the Keystone Trails Association at our website or telephone 717-238-7017. (The Appalachian Trail Conservancy's website lists the clubs' websites in the Trail clubs section (www.appalachiantrail.org).

Allentown Hiking Club   www.allentownhikingclub.org

Appalachian Mountain Club   www.amcdv.org
Delaware Valley Chapter

BATONA Hiking Club   www.batonahikingclub.org

Blue Mountain Eagle   www.bmecc.org
Climbing Club

Cumberland Valley A.T. Club   www.cvatclub.org

Mountain Club of Maryland   www.mcomd.org

Philadelphia Trail Club   http://m.zanger.tripod.com

Potomac Appalachian Trail Club   www.patc.net
North Chapter

Susquehanna Appalachian   www.satc-hike.org
Trail Club

Wilmington Trail Club

                                              www.wilmingtontrailclub.org

York Hiking Club   www.yorkhikingclub.com

PENNSYLVANIA APPALACHIAN TRAIL
MAINTENANCE ASSIGNMENTS

Maintaining Organization	Club Mileage	Miles*	Boundary Feature
		0.0	Delaware Water Gap
Wilmington Trail Club	7.2		
		7.2	Fox Gap
BATONA Hiking Club	8.6		
		15.8	Wind Gap
AMC - Del Valley Chapter	15.4		
		31.2	Little Gap
Philadelphia Trail Club	10.3		
		41.5	Lehigh Furnace Gap
BMECC	3.4	44.9	Bake Oven Knob Road
Allentown Hiking Club	10.3		
		55.2	Tri-County Corner
Blue Mountain Eagle Climbing Club (BMECC)	62.5		
		117.7	Rausch Gap Shelter
Susquehanna A.T. Club	20.8		
		138.5	Pa. Rt. 225
York Hiking Club	7.2		
		145.7	Susquehanna River
Mountain Club of Maryland	12.7		
		158.4	Darlington Trail
Cumberland Valley A.T. Club	17.2		
		175.6	Center Point Knob
Mountain Club of Maryland	16.7		
		192.3	Pine Grove Furnace
Potomac Appalachian Trail Club - North Chapter	37.4		
		229.7	Pen Mar

* Miles are cumulative from N to S

64

MEASUREMENTS

Distances in this guide book are given in traditional units; e.g., miles, yards, feet. For the benefit of those readers who may be interested, a metric conversion table is printed near the front of this book.

TRAIL MARKINGS

On some highways, the point where the Appalachian Trail crosses is marked by a large brown wood signboard. About 100 have been erected by the Pennsylvania Department of Transportation as a public service.

The Trail is marked by white rectangular paint blazes on trees, power or telephone poles, and occasionally on rocks. The standard size for paint blazes is two inches wide by six inches long. Blazes are applied in a vertical position. The paint blazes are at frequent intervals, and hikers should have no difficulty following the Trail if they watch for the blazes.

A "double blaze" (two blazes, one above the other with a space between) is placed as a warning sign. It may indicate an obscure turn or change in direction which might not otherwise be noticed; or it may indicate a change in trail conditions, such as difficult footing.

A hiker should not go more than a quarter of a mile without seeing a blaze or other Trail indication. If this happens, retrace your steps until you again encounter blazes. Then proceed with caution. Recent timbering operations may have created complications. In such areas, use extreme caution. Trail relocations are normally indicated by signs. Blue blazes indicate a side trail to a spring, viewpoint, shelter, or an access trail.

The yellow blazes of the Horse-Shoe Trail are seen only at its junction with the Appalachian Trail north of Harrisburg. Blue blazes are used for the Tuscarora Trail. Other colors are used on other trails. State Game Land and State Forest boundaries are marked with non-uniform white and yellow blazes which can be confusing to hikers. Hikers should be aware that boundaries could be painted with white or yellow paint and are deliberately not neat. Use caution.

SHELTERS AND CABINS

Open three- or four-sided shelters are located along the Trail at varying distances. A spring or other water source and a privy are usually nearby.

The shelters were constructed for the benefit of hikers, not for picnickers. All hikers may use them on a "first-come first-served" basis and for one night only. They should be shared to the limit of their capacity. Be hospitable, courteous, clean, and neat. Shelters are built and maintained by volunteers. They spend a lot of time and money in this endeavor. You are responsible not to damage the shelter and to leave a clean camp. Burn or take home all refuse and tin cans. If you carry it in, you carry it out. Please practice Leave No Trace principles.

A number of shelters have composting privies. These privies are installed and maintained by volunteers at a considerable expense. Garbage and trash must not be placed into the privy and liquid waste should be minimized for these privies to work effectively. For everyone's enjoyment, please cooperate.

Unfortunately certain shelters have proven to be highly attractive to vandals. All shelter users are encouraged to do whatever they can to encourage respect for these structures and to help reduce the level of vandalism and abuse.

In the division south of the Susquehanna River are four three locked cabins managed by the Potomac Appalachian Trail Club. To use these cabins, reservations must be made in advance at PATC's Headquarters, 118 Park Street, S.E., Vienna, VA 22180-4609 or online at www.potomacappalachian.com. Keys will be supplied for definite dates and a fee is charged for the use of these cabins.

MAPS

Keystone Trails Association publishes the maps for the portion of the A.T. between the Delaware Water Gap and the Susquehanna River. The maps are designed for use with this guidebook. For a current price list, contact KTA at 717-238-7017 or www.kta-hike.org.

The Potomac Appalachian Trail Club publishes the maps for the portion of the A.T. between the Susquehanna River and Pen Mar. These can be used in connection with this guidebook. They can be ordered from KTA or PATC.

The above maps are also available from Appalachian Trail Conservancy headquarters (Telephone: 888-AT-STORE or web: www.appalachiantrail.org) and, during weekday office hours, at the Mid-Atlantic Regional Office in Boiling Springs.

For those desiring more detailed topographic information, the USGS 7 1/2' quadrangle maps are available. They can be purchased from the U.S. Geological Survey, Box 25046, Denver Federal Center, Building 810, Denver, CO 80225. The appropriate quadrangles for the Appalachian Trail are listed below. It is important to note that the A.T. may or may not be shown on these maps, and that when shown, may not be accurate because of the relocations that have occurred over the years. It is suggested that if these maps are to be used, the actual route should be transferred to them from current KTA maps.

Detailed maps and other publications about the geology of the Trail in Pennsylvania are shown in a free "List of Publications," which is available from: PA Department of Natural Resources and Conservation, Bureau of Topographic and Geologic Survey, 3240 Schoolhouse Road, Middletown, PA 17057-3534 or online at www.dcnr.state.pa.us/topogeo/pub/ordering.aspx.

PA. A.T. SECTIONS	USGS QUADRANGLES
Delaware Water Gap to Lehigh Gap	Stroudsburg Saylorsburg Wind Gap Kunkletown Palmerton

Lehigh Gap to Schuylkill Gap	Palmerton Lehighton Slatedale New Tripoli New Ringgold Hamburg Auburn
Schuylkill Gap to Swatara Gap	Auburn Friedensburg Swatara Hill Pine Grove Fredericksburg Indiantown Gap
Swatara Gap to Susquehanna River	Indiantown Gap Tower City Grantville Enders Halifax Duncannon
Susquehanna River to Pa. Rt. 94	Duncannon Wertzville Mechanicsburg Dillsburg Mt. Holly Springs
Pa. Rt. 94 to Caledonia	Mt. Holly Springs Dickinson Walnut Bottom Caledonia Park
Caledonia to Pen Mar	Caledonia Park Iron Springs Waynesboro Blue Ridge Summit Smithburg

SUGGESTIONS FOR HIKERS

TRANSPORTATION

Private shuttlers are available for hire. A current list of them and their areas of coverage is maintained on the Appalachian Trail Conservancy's website - www.appalachiantrail.org.

DAY HIKES AND SHORT HIKES

There are several areas along the A.T. in Pennsylvania that provide opportunities for day hikes and short backpacking trips utilizing the A.T. side trails and connecting trails. These trails are shown on the A.T. maps for Pennsylvania, and many of the side trails are described in this guide. These trail systems and the hikes using them are described in more detail in *Pennsylvania Hiking Trails*; Keystone Trails Association: Thirteenth edition; 2008. Order from KTA.

Some areas along the Pennsylvania A.T. that may be of interest for shorter hikes are listed below, along with the identifying Section number in each case:

- The Delaware Water Gap. Section 1
- The Pinnacle, Windsor Furnace, and Hawk Mountain Sanctuary. Section 4.
- St. Anthony's Wilderness, State Game Lands 210 and 211. Section 7.
- Pole Steeple area. Section 12.
- Pine Grove Furnace area. Sections 12 and 13.
- Caledonia State Park area. Section 13.

SUMMARY OF DISTANCES

MILES N. to S. (Section)	MILES N. to S. (Cumulative)	Trail Feature	MILES S. to N. (Section)	MILES S. to N. (Cumulative)
		Section 1		
0.0	0.0	I-80, Delaware River Bridge	15.8	229.7
4.8	4.8	Totts Gap	11.0	224.9
6.5	6.5	Kirkridge Shelter	9.3	223.2
7.2	7.2	Fox Gap, Rt. 191	8.6	222.5
8.8	8.8	Wolf Rocks	7.0	220.9
15.8	15.8	Wind Gap	0.0	213.9
		Section 2		
0.0	15.8	Wind Gap	20.7	213.9
4.6	20.4	L.A. Smith Shelter	16.1	209.3
8.1	23.9	Smith Gap	12.6	205.8
15.4	31.2	Little Gap	5.3	198.5
20.7	36.5	Lehigh Gap, Rts 248 & 873	0.0	193.2
		Section 3		
0.0	36.5	Lehigh Gap, Rts 248 & 873	13.3	193.2
0.6	37.1	Outerbridge Shelter	12.7	192.6
5.0	41.5	Lehigh Furnace Gap/Ashfield Rd.	8.3	188.2
7.4	43.9	Bake Oven Knob Shelter	5.9	185.8
8.4	44.9	Bake Oven Knob Road	4.9	184.8
11.5	48.0	New Tripoli Campsite	1.8	181.7
13.3	49.8	Blue Mountain Summit, Rt. 309	0.0	179.9
		Section 4		
0.0	49.8	Blue Mountain Summit, Rt. 309	26.7	179.9
2.2	52.0	Fort Franklin Rd.	24.5	177.7
4.1	53.9	Allentown Shelter	22.6	175.8
5.4	55.2	Tri-County Corner	21.3	174.5
11.5	61.3	Eckville Shelter	15.2	168.4
16.8	66.6	The Pinnacle	9.9	163.1
17.2	67.0	Trail to Blue Rocks Campground	9.5	162.7
20.6	70.4	Windsor Furnace Shelter	6.1	159.3
23.4	73.2	Pocahontas Spring	3.3	156.5
26.7	76.5	Port Clinton, Rt. 61	0.0	153.2

MILES N. to S. (Section)	MILES N. to S. (Cumulative)	Trail Feature	MILES S. to N. (Section)	MILES S. to N. (Cumulative)
		Section 5		
0.0	76.5	Port Clinton, RR Bridge	14.4	153.2
8.6	85.1	Eagles Nest Shelter	5.8	144.6
14.4	90.9	Rt. 183	0.0	138.8
		Section 6		
0.0	90.9	Rt. 183	20.7	138.8
3.7	94.6	Hertlein Campsite	17.0	135.1
6.2	97.1	Round Head/Showers Steps Trail	14.5	132.6
9.3	100.2	Rt. 501 Shelter	11.4	129.5
13.4	104.3	William Penn Shelter	7.3	125.4
20.7	111.6	Swatara Gap	0.0	118.1
		Section 7		
0.0	111.6	Swatara Gap	17.4	118.1
6.1	117.7	Rausch Gap Shelter	11.3	112.0
10.7	122.3	Yellow Springs Village	6.7	107.4
17.4	129.0	Clarks Valley, Rt. 325	0.0	100.7
		Section 8		
0.0	129.0	Clarks Valley, Rt. 325	16.7	100.7
6.7	135.7	Peters Mountain Shelter	10.0	94.0
9.5	138.5	Rt. 225	7.2	91.2
13.4	142.4	Clarks Ferry Shelter	3.3	87.3
16.7	145.7	Clarks Ferry Bridge	0.0	84.0
		Section 9		
0.0	145.7	Clarks Ferry Bridge	14.6	84.0
5.3	151.0	Cove Mountain Shelter	9.3	78.7
10.3	156.0	Rt. 850	4.3	73.7
12.6	158.3	Darlington Shelter	2.0	71.4
14.6	160.3	Rt. 944	0.0	69.4
		Section 10		
0.0	160.3	Rt. 944	12.3	69.4
4.3	164.6	U.S. Rt. 11	8.0	65.1
10.3	170.6	Rt. 74	2.0	59.1
12.0	172.3	Rt. 174	0.3	57.4
12.3	172.6	Boiling Springs	0.0	57.1

MILES N. to S. (Section)	MILES N. to S. (Cumulative)	Trail Feature	MILES S. to N. (Section)	MILES S. to N. (Cumulative)
		Section 11		
0.0	172.6	Boiling Springs	8.8	57.1
3.0	175.6	Center Point Knob	5.8	54.1
3.9	176.5	Alec Kennedy Shelter	4.9	53.2
6.0	178.6	Whiskey Spring Road	2.8	51.1
8.8	181.4	Rt. 94	0.0	48.3
		Section 12		
0.0	181.4	Rt. 94	10.9	48.3
1.8	183.2	Rt. 34	9.1	46.5
2.9	184.3	Hunters Run Road	8.0	45.4
3.2	184.6	Tagg Run Shelter	7.7	45.1
10.9	192.3	Pine Grove Furnace State Park, Rt. 233	0.0	37.4
		Section 13		
0.0	192.3	Pine Grove Furnace State Park, Rt. 233	19.5	37.4
2.1	194.4	Michaux Road	17.4	35.3
3.4	195.7	Toms Run Shelters	16.1	34.0
8.3	200.6	Arendtsville-Shippensburg Rd.	11.2	29.1
9.7	202.0	Birch Run Shelters	9.8	27.7
12.1	204.4	Milesburn Cabin	7.4	25.3
17.0	209.3	Quarry Gap Shelters	2.5	20.4
19.5	211.8	Caledonia State Park, Rt. 30	0.0	17.9
		Section 14		
0.0	211.8	Caledonia State Park, Rt. 30	17.9	17.9
3.0	214.8	Rocky Mountain Shelters	14.9	14.9
8.3	220.1	Hermitage Cabin	9.6	9.6
9.6	221.4	Tumbling Run Shelters	8.3	8.3
10.8	222.6	Antietam Shelter	7.1	7.1
13.2	225.0	Deer Lick Shelters	4.7	4.7
15.3	227.1	Rt. 16	2.6	2.6
17.9	229.7	Pen Mar	0.0	0.0

Halfway Marker © Ernest Yeagley

SECTION ONE

DELAWARE WATER GAP TO WIND GAP

DISTANCE: 15.8 Mi.

This section of Trail is maintained from the Delaware River to Fox G
by the Wilmington Trail Club and from Fox Gap to Wind Gap by
BATONA Hiking Club.

OVERVIEW OF SECTION 1

From an elevation of 300 ft. at the Delaware River, the Trail clim
gradually for 2.7 mi. to Mt. Minsi at 1,461 ft. with panoramic views of t
Delaware River below, Mt. Tammany across the river, and Dunnfie
Creek where the A.T. ascends the mountain across the river in New Jers
The Trail in the Delaware Water Gap ascends through beautiful hemlo
and rhododendron. The Trail follows a ridge with slight dips into To
Gap and Fox Gap and a deeper one into Wind Gap. From early summer c
this whole section is lacking in good springs. Points of interest along t
Trail are Lake Lenape, Council Rock, Lookout Rock, Mt. Minsi, Lun
Rocks, and Wolf Rocks. In the Wolf Rocks area use care and follow t
blazes. The mountain top at this point is nearly one mile wide and t
Trail, once lost, is difficult to find. Wolf Rocks consists of massi
jumbled boulders covered with rock tripe and other lichens.

GENERAL INFORMATION

MAPS

Use KTA Sections 1-6 Map. This section of trail is on the following USC
7 1/2' quads: Stroudsburg, Saylorsburg, and Wind Gap.

SHELTERS AND DESIGNATED CAMPSITES

6.5 mi   from the Delaware Water Gap is Kirkridge Shelter. Water is available in season from an outside tap on a blue-blazed trail toward the Kirkridge Retreat.

PUBLIC ACCOMMODATIONS

In Delaware Water Gap village there are motels, hotels, and restaurants. The Presbyterian Church of the Mountain, located just north of the Trail on Main Street, provides a hostel and information center for hikers. In Wind Gap, lodging may be obtained at the Gateway Motel, 100 yards north of the Gap. Water is available for thru-hikers. Lodging and restaurants are located in Wind Gap Borough down the south side of the mountain.

SUPPLIES

Supplies can be obtained at several places in Delaware Water Gap Borough. The Pack Shack offers backpacking equipment and clothing, as well as repair services for equipment hikers carry. Supplies can be obtained at several places in Wind Gap Borough.

Trail Maintenance © Allen Britton

DELAWARE WATER GAP

In the Borough of Delaware Water Gap there are motels, hotels, and restaurants. Packages can be mailed at the post office (ZIP Code 18327). The Presbyterian Church of the Mountain, located just north of the Trail on Main Street, provides a hostel and information center for hikers. Bus service is available from Martz Trailways; call 800-223-8604. Supplies can be obtained at several places in Delaware Water Gap Borough. The Pack Shack offers backpacking equipment and clothing, as well as repair services for equipment hikers carry.

Mile point 0.0 at the Delaware River on the Pennsylvania side of the Interstate 80 bridge cannot be reached from I-80, since parking on the bridge is not possible. Enter Delaware Water Gap village on Pa. Rt. 61. At the intersection of Main Street and Mountain Road a large PennDOT sign notes the A.T. which comes in from I-80 on Delaware Avenue. The street dead ends at the chain barrier on I-80 opposite a red brick highway maintenance building between the toll house and the bridge. A parking lot for hikers is located along the Trail 0.3 mi. south of the bridge.

FRED WARING

The street is named after Fredrick Waring, a Pennsylvania native, who was known as the "The Man Who Taught America How to Sing". He attended Pennsylvania State University studying Architectural Engineering. In the 1920s his "Waring's Pennsylvanians" were among the top record selling bands. He financed the development of what became the Waring Blendor. For almost 40 years he held choral workshops at Shawnee-on-Delaware and home to his Shawnee Press, Inc. After a lifetime of radio, recording and television music he was awarded the Congressional Gold Medal.

CHERRY VALLEY NATIONAL WILDLIFE REFUGE

Compass north of the Appalachian Trail from the Delaware Water Gap approximately 3 mi. south of Wind Gap is 20,466 acres of land that was designated as the Cherry Creek National Wildlife Refuge on December 2, 2008 by the US Fish and Wildlife Service. The refuge is home to 85 rare species. The Service will begin the process of land protection and purchase of land from willing sellers.

N-S	**Trail Description**	S-N

0.0   **Delaware Water Gap** The northern end of this section   15.8
is the PA end of the Interstate 80 Bridge over Delaware
River along the sidewalk on the PA side of the bridge.

Southbound Hikers: Bear left on a path a short distance
south of the toll plaza to end of Delaware Avenue. In
one block, turn left onto Waring Drive and follow it for
50 ft. to Pa. Rt. 611.

Northbound Hikers: Cross bridge over Delaware River
into New Jersey (see *The Appalachian Trail Guide to
New York – New Jersey*).

0.2   Cross Pa. Rt. 611 (Main Street).   15.6

Southbound Hikers: Continue uphill on Mountain Road.

Northbound Hikers: Continue on **Waring** Drive for 50
ft. Turn right onto Delaware Street and follow trail to
Interstate 80 Bridge.

0.3   Intersection of paved Lake Road and Mountain Road.   15.5

0.4   Pass hikers parking lot.   15.4

0.6   Pass Lake Lenape. A blue-blazed side trail on the east   15.2
side reconnects with the A.T. at 0.8/15.0 mi.

0.7   A.T. intersection with gravel road. The gravel road leads   15.1
up the mountain and to a side trail to Table Rock with a
view of the Water Gap.

Southbound Hikers: For the next two miles follow
blazes carefully because there are many unmarked trails
branching off the A.T.

DELAWARE WATER GAP NATIONAL RECREATION AREA →

With over 70,000 acres, the Delaware Water Gap National Recreation Area is the largest NRA in the east. With close proximity to a large portion of the nation's population it is one of the most visited units of the National Park System. The U.S. Army Corps of Engineers acquired land displaced many families living on farms along the river and destroyed many homes to build a dam at Tocks Island that would have inundated 30 mi. of the Delaware River and 30,000 acres. The defeat of the dam was a major grass roots environmental success. The main stem of the Delaware River is longest stretch of a river without a dam east of the Mississippi River.

CHIEF TAMMANY →

Chief Tammany, chief of the Lenni Lenape Native Americans, lived in the 17th century. He, with William Penn, founder of Pennsylvania, conceived an agreement in 1683 where Europeans and Indians would live together in peace. Chief Tammany was considered a great man among white people.

POCONO PLATEAU →

The Pocono Plateau is a previously glaciated mountain plateau in northeastern Pennsylvania. The plateau has unique boreal wetlands home to one of the most reproductive populations of black bears in the country, native river otters, snowshoe hare, bobcat, river otters, dozens of species of rare moths and butterflies. Municipal and county referendum supporting open space protection have been enacted to protect the area. In addition, the Nature Conservancy has named the Pocono Plateau as one of the world's "Last Great Places" and has purchased over 14,000 acres of land.

BIG POCONO →

Big Pocono at elevation 2,132 feet above sea level in Big Pocono State Park provides excellent views of the surrounding Poconos, the length of the Appalachian Trail from High Point State Park in New Jersey to Lehigh Gap in Pennsylvania, and the Catskills in New York.

N-S	**Trail Description**	S-N

0.9   Council Rock.   Down the Delaware River, the tilted   14.9
strata of Mount Tammany on the left side of "The Gap"
is said to show the profile of **Chief Tammany**.

1.5   Cross Eureka Creek.   14.3

1.7   Side trail to east to Lookout Rock and view of Delaware   14.1
River and Delaware Water Gap.

1.9   A view north to the **Pocono Plateau** and **Big Pocono**.   13.9

2.4   Panoramic view of the Delaware Water Gap and the   13.4
surrounding area of Pennsylvania and New Jersey.

2.7   Summit of Mt. Minsi at 1,461 ft.   13.1

    Southbound Hikers: A.T. follows a gravel road along
the crest.

    Northbound Hikers: Begin descent.

2.8   Trail to east side of A.T. leads 100 ft to view south   13.0
overlooking the Delaware Valley.

4.2   Southbound Hikers: Trail turns left into woods.   11.6

    Northbound Hikers: Trail turns right onto gravel road.

4.4   Cross pipeline right-of-way.   11.4

4.7   Tott's Gap.   11.1

    Southbound Hikers: Cross dirt road and ascend over
rocks.

    Northbound Hikers: Cross dirt road. Trail bears right
into woods passing communications towers.

Delaware Water Gap Road Crossing
© Thomas Scully

KIRKRIDGE SHELTER →

Water is available in season from an outside tap on a blue-blazed trail toward the Kirkridge Retreat. Follow the blue-blazed trail. Please respect the privacy of those at the retreat center and do not trespass. Excellent view to the south. Shelter was re-built in 2006.

FOX GAP →

Pa. Rt. 191 crosses between Bangor and Stroudsburg. A small parking area is located here.

N-S	**<u>Trail Description</u>**	S-N

4.9	Cross twin power lines with views to the north.	10.9
5.8	Reach Lunch Rocks 50 ft on east with a view north along the ridge into New Jersey.	10.0
6.4	Nelson's Overlook. Good views to South.	9.4
6.5	Blue-blazed trail (North end), which leads to the **Kirkridge Shelter,** connects with A.T.	9.3
6.6	Blue-blazed trail (South end), which leads to the **Kirkridge Shelter,** connects with A.T.	9.2
6.8	Cross orange-blazed trail known as "The Great Walk", which descends mountain 0.8 mi. to a replica of an early Celtic Christian Church.	9.0
7.1	Bulletin Board at green-blazed cross trail.	8.7
7.2	Cross Pa. Rt. 191 in **Fox Gap**. Cross the road cautiously.	8.6
8.1	Trail turns. Southbound Hikers: Turn right, joining woods road flanked by stone walls. Northbound Hikers: Turn left, leaving woods road.	7.7
8.6	Pass under a power line. Trail turns. Southbound Hikers: Turn left, leaving woods road. Northbound Hikers: Turn right, joining woods road flanked by stone walls.	7.2

Lake Lenape © Wayne E. Gross

WIND GAP ➔

In Wind Gap, the Trail can be reached via the Wind Gap-Saylorsburg Road (North Broadway Road) which passes under Pa. Rt. 33. The Trail is visible from Pa. Rt. 33 (a limited access highway) but can be reached only from North Broadway Road. A small parking area is located adjacent to the A.T. sign on the north side of North Broadway Road where the A.T. crosses the road.

In Wind Gap, lodging may be obtained at the Gateway Motel, 100 yards compass north of the Gap. Water is available for thru-hikers. Lodging, restaurants and post office (ZIP Code 18091) are located in Wind Gap Borough down the south side of the mountain. Supplies can be obtained at several places in Wind Gap Borough.

N-S	**Trail Description**	S-N

8.8   Reach Wolf Rocks with impressive views of Big Pocono   7.0
        and the Pocono Plateau to the north. Follow the top
        edge of the rocks.

        Southbound Hikers: Use care to follow blazes in the next
        5 mi. Once lost, the Trail in this area is difficult to find.

13.7   Trail crosses a private road of the Blue Mountain Water   2.1
        Company affording a view.

        Northbound Hikers: Use care to follow blazes in the next
        5 mi. Once lost, the Trail in this area is difficult to find.

15.8   Intersection with North Broadway Road from Borough   0.0
        of **Wind Gap** Borough just south of Pa. Rt. 33.

        Southbound Hikers: Continue on A.T. by turning right
        at official Appalachian Trail signboard. Cross North
        Broadway Road and pass below the overpass carrying
        Pa. Rt. 33, a limited access highway.   This can be a
        dangerous road crossing due to fast moving traffic at
        times. Caution is advised.

        Northbound Hikers: Begin ascent up mountain out of the
        gap.

SECTION 2

WIND GAP TO LEHIGH GAP

DISTANCE: 20.7 Mi.

This section of Trail is maintained by the Delaware Valley Chapter of the Appalachian Mountain Club from Wind Gap to Little Gap, and by the Philadelphia Trail Club from Little Gap to Lehigh Gap.

OVERVIEW OF SECTION 2

The Trail is in State Game Lands most of the way, where overnight camping is permitted. (See introductory section on Pennsylvania Game Commission.) After climbing out of Wind Gap, and passing Hahn's Lookout, the Trail stays on the ridge crossing Smith Gap until the dip and climb in Little Gap. From there, it traverses an open rocky area which allows views of the railroads and Palmerton, industrial home of New Jersey Zinc Company. Be sure to carry plenty of water since springs in the entire section are apt to be dry by early June most years. Part of Blue Mountain north of Lehigh Gap is in the 10 mile diameter Palmerton EPA Superfund Site caused by the zinc smelters that used to operate near Palmerton. The U.S. Public Health Service has advised that hiking this portion of the A.T. does not represent a public health threat.

GENERAL INFORMATION

MAPS

Use KTA Sections 1-6 Map. This section of trail is on the following USGS 7.5' quadrangles: Wind Gap, Kunkletown, and Palmerton.

SHELTERS AND DESIGNATED CAMPSITES

4.6 mi   from Wind Gap is Leroy A. Smith Shelter built by the AMC Delaware Valley Chapter in 1972. The spring is 0.3 mi. south past shelter on side trail.

PUBLIC ACCOMMODATIONS

Wind Gap. Lodging may be obtained at the Gateway Motel, 100 yds. north of the gap. Water is available to thru-hikers.

Palmerton. The Borough allows hikers to sleep in the basement of the Borough Hall with the use of showers at no charge. Hikers should check in at the Borough office before 4:30 PM. You will need to provide name, ID, address, trail name, and social security number. 443 Delaware Ave. 540-826-2286 There is a locked fence gate at end of blue-blazed Winter Trail. Plan to be through the gate by 4:30 PM. See trail description for details.

Slatington. Fine Lodging, 700 Main Street (Pa. Rt. 873), Slatington, Pa. 18080-0002. Possibility of hiker pick-up at Trail; call 610-760-0700. Can be used for mail drop. Slatington also has laundromats, banks (with ATM machines), a post office, grocery stores, and 24-hour convenience stores.

Restaurants are available in Wind Gap, Danielsville, Palmerton, Walnutport, and Slatington.

SUPPLIES

Supplies can be obtained in Wind Gap, Danielsville, Palmerton, Walnutport, and Slatington.

WIND GAP →

In Wind Gap, the Trail can be reached via the Wind Gap-Saylorsburg Road (North Broadway Road) which passes under Pa. Rt. 33. The Trail is visible from Pa. Rt. 33 (a limited access highway) but can be reached only from North Broadway Road. A small parking area is located adjacent to the A.T. sign on the north side of North Broadway Road where the A.T. crosses the road.

In Wind Gap, lodging may be obtained at the Gateway Motel, 100 yards north of the Gap. Water is available for thru-hikers. Lodging, restaurants and post office (ZIP Code 18091) are located in Wind Gap Borough down the south side of the mountain. Supplies can be obtained at several places in Wind Gap Borough.

LEROY A. SMITH SHELTER →

Springs at 0.2, 0.4, and 0.5 mi. The third spring is reliable year round. Paved road at 0.9 mi.

Leroy A. Smith Shelter © Charles Olge

N-S	**Trail Description**	S-N

0.0   Intersection with North Broadway Road from   20.7
Borough of **Wind Gap** Borough just south of Pa.
Rt. 33.

Southbound Hikers: Continue on A.T. by turning
right at official Appalachian Trail signboard, passing
below the overpass carrying Pa. Rt. 33, a limited
access highway.

Northbound Hikers: Continue on A.T. by turning
right and pass below the overpass carrying Pa. Rt.
33, a limited access highway. Cross North
Broadway Road to A.T. sign and parking lot. This
can be a dangerous road crossing due to fast moving
traffic at times. Caution is advised.

0.3   Cross power line.   20.4

0.8   Lookout Rock. Views north over Saylorsburg, with   19.9
Poconos in distance, and Aquashicola Creek in
Chestnut Valley in foreground.

Southbound Hikers: From here, Trail bears left to
traverse the south side of Blue Mountain.

Northbound Hikers: Trail descends by switchbacks.

1.0   Hahn's Lookout. View south of Wind Gap Borough   19.6
and South Mountain in the distance.

2.7   Cross underground pipeline.   17.9

4.4   Cross transmission line to tower. Good views north.   16.2

4.6   Pass blue-blazed Katellen Trail on east. **Leroy A.**   16.0
Smith Shelter at 0.14 mi.

SMITH GAP ROAD➔

Smith Gap Road crosses from Point Phillip to Kunkletown. The road is paved from compass north. From compass south the gravel road is steep with sharp turns and may be hazardous in snowy conditions. Very limited parking on NPS lands.

SUPERFUND SITE ➔

Efforts to remediate environmental damage in the Superfund site started along the top of the ridge in 2008. The footpath between the Winter Trail-A.T. junction at the top of Lehigh Gap and Little Gap has been relocated to accommodate this activity. This relocation is temporary and is partially on private property on the north side of the ridge. It is anticipated that the Trail will be moved to a permanent alignment wholly on public lands in the future.

LITTLE GAP ➔

In Little Gap the A.T. crosses Blue Mountain Road. Compass south 1.5 mi. is Danielsville and Pa. Rt. 946. Compass north is the village of Little Gap. A State Game Lands parking lot is in the gap about 0.1 mi. east of the Trail.

The footpath between Little Gap and the intersection with blue-blazed Winter Trail at mileage 19.3/1.4 is a temporary relocation done in 2008. A permanent alignment will be designed in the future.

N-S	**Trail Description**	S-N
8.1	Cross **Smith Gap Road**.	12.5
10.6	Blue-blazed Delps Trail on east (1.1 mi. to road). Very unreliable spring 0.3 mi. down side trail.	10.1
11.6	Cross power line.	9.0
12.0	Blue-blazed trail on the east leads to overlook in 130 yds. NO camping within view of the overlook.	8.6
15.1	Weathering Knob. Views north.	5.6
15.4	Cross Blue Mountain Road in **Little Gap**. Southbound Hikers: Bear slight left, cross pipeline. Northbound Hikers: Trail crosses bog, then up steep talus slope.	5.3
15.5	Information board and register. Southbound Hikers: Follow footpath uphill through woods. Northbound Hikers: Follow footpath downhill through woods.	5.2
16.0	Edge of old road.	4.7
16.6	Cross under high-tension wires.	4.1
17.5	Southbound Hikers: Descend stairs and bear left onto grassy lane. Continuous open views for next two miles. Northbound Hikers: Bear right off of grassy lane and ascend stairs.	3.2

LEHIGH GAP →

In Lehigh Gap, this section begins at the compass west end of the Pa. Rt. 873 bridge over the Lehigh River, two miles compass south of Palmerton. The east end is private property. Use the hiker parking lot on the old railroad bed accessible from a small entry road compass east of the Pa. Rt. 248 traffic light. Additional parking is also available at the Lehigh Gap Nature Center (access road below bridge), and a side trail connects from there to the A.T.

In order to walk to Palmerton, from the southern junction of the A.T. and Winter Trail, follow the blue-blazed Winter Trail. Where the Winter Trail turns right uphill, continue straight ahead on the railroad bed and eventually descend in about 0.5 mi. to a fenced in parking lot with a private gated bridge crossing Aquashicola Creek at opposite end of the parking lot. The fence gate is locked after 4:30 PM. If you are granted permission to cross the bridge, cross and resume walk on other side on paved Red Hill Drive into Palmerton. If access to private bridge is not possible, backtrack through the parking lot, climb over guardrail onto Pa. Rt. 248. Please use extreme care along road and cross highway bridge on shoulder of road, then cross over guardrail again to Red Hill Drive and follow it into Palmerton. It is recommended that you plan to get through the fence gate prior to 4:30 PM.

N-S	**Trail Description**	S-N
18.7	Edge of old road. Views north.	2.0
19.3	Intersect blue-blazed Winter Trail (The Winter Trail is an alternate route to A.T. for descending into Lehigh Gap. It rejoins the A.T. in 1.5 mi. at mileage 20.3/0.4 in the valley. This is a less difficult route.)	1.4
19.5	Cross a shoulder of the Blue Mountain with fine views of the valley. Rocky area.	1.2
	Southbound Hikers: Descend steeply. Cross a rocky slide area of the ridge with continuous views, but extreme exposure to adverse weather. Watch carefully for blazes on rocks.	
20.3	Turn at sign. The blue-blazed Winter Trail continues on the rail bed and rejoins the A.T. in 1.5 mi. at mileage 19.3/1.4. This is a less difficult route.	0.4
	Southbound Hikers: Descend to Pa. Rt. 248. Bear left to the traffic light.	
20.4	Cross Pa. Rt. 248	0.3
20.6	Cross Pa. Rt. 873 bridge across the Lehigh River.	0.1
20.7	**Lehigh Gap**	0.0
	Southbound Hikers: At west end of Pa. Rt. 873 bridge, turn right and carefully cross highway. Trail will continue up hill.	
	Northbound Hikers: Cross Pa. Rt. 248 at the traffic light, where it junctions with Pa. Rt. 145. Turn left along Pa. Rt. 248 for 150 feet. Turn right up embankment. Cross old railbed.	

SECTION 3

LEHIGH GAP TO PA. RT. 309

DISTANCE: 13.3 Mi.

This section of the Trail is maintained by the Philadelphia Trail Club from Lehigh Gap to Lehigh Furnace Gap; by the Blue Mountain Eagle Climbing Club from Lehigh Furnace Gap to Bake Oven Knob Road; and by the Allentown Hiking Club from Bake Oven Knob Road to Pa. Rt. 309.

OVERVIEW OF SECTION 3

The Trail climbs steadily to the Outerbridge Shelter, beyond which the A.T. continues to the ridge top with scenic views but open to winter storms. A point of interest off the Trail is Devil's Pulpit, overlooking the Lehigh River. The A.T. then passes through State Game Lands and dips to Lehigh Furnace Gap. State Game Lands boundary blazes are often confused with A.T. blazes but are of erratic size and location. USE CAUTION. Climbing again, the Trail leads to Bake Oven Knob with its commanding view of fertile farmland below, and its reputation as a birdwatcher's vantage point during the fall hawk migrations. The Trail passes Bear Rocks with 360 degree views, and then crosses a knife edge rocks known as "The Cliffs." This is one of the most scenic sections of the A.T. in Pennsylvania.

GENERAL INFORMATION

MAPS

Use KTA Sections 1-6 Map. This section of trail is on the following USGS 7 1/2' quads: Palmerton, Lehighton, Slatedale, and New Tripoli.

SHELTERS AND DESIGNATED CAMPSITES

0.6 mi.   from Lehigh Gap is the George W. Outerbridge Shelter, located directly along the Trail. Spring is passed before reaching shelter.

7.4 mi.   from Lehigh Gap is the Bake Oven Knob shelter, located just south of the Trail. Variable springs are located down the hill on a blue-blazed trail at 100 yds., 200 yds, and a third further down the mountain.

PUBLIC ACCOMMODATIONS

Palmerton. The Borough allows hikers to sleep in the basement of the Borough Hall with the use of showers at no charge. Hikers should check in at the Borough office before 4:30 PM. You will need to provide name, ID, address, trail name, and social security number. 443 Delaware Ave. 540-826-2286

Slatington. Fine Lodging, 700 Main Street (Pa. Rt. 873), Slatington, PA 18080-0002. Possibility of hiker pick-up at Trail; call 610-760-0700. Can be used for mail drop. Slatington also has laundromats, banks (with ATM machines), a post office, grocery stores, and 24-hour convenience stores.

Restaurants are also available in Palmerton and Slatington.

SUPPLIES

Supplies can be obtained in nearby Palmerton, Walnutport, Ashfield and Slatington.

LEHIGH GAP →

In Lehigh Gap, this section begins at the compass west end of the Pa. Rt. 873 bridge over the Lehigh River, two miles compass south of Palmerton. The east end is private property. Use the hiker parking lot on the old railroad bed accessible from a small entry road compass east of the Pa. Rt. 248 traffic light. Additional parking is also available at the Lehigh Gap Nature Center (access road below bridge), and a side trail connects from there to the A.T.

In order to walk to Palmerton, from the southern junction of the A.T. and Winter Trail, follow the blue-blazed Winter Trail. Where the Winter Trail turns right uphill, continue straight ahead on the railroad bed and eventually descend in about 0.5 mi. to a fenced in parking lot with a private gated bridge crossing Aquashicola Creek at opposite end of the parking lot. The fence gate is locked after 4:30 PM. If you are granted permission to cross the bridge, cross and resume walk on other side on paved Red Hill Drive into Palmerton. If access to private bridge is not possible, backtrack through the parking lot, climb over guardrail onto Pa. Rt. 248. Please use extreme care along road and cross highway bridge on shoulder of road, then cross over guardrail again to Red Hill Drive and follow it into Palmerton. It is recommended that you plan to get through the fence gate prior to 4:30 PM.

GEORGE W. OUTERBRIDGE SHELTER →

George W. Outerbridge Shelter is along the A.T. on west. A piped spring is along the Trail 105 yards north of the shelter. George W. Outerbridge was the first person to section hike the entire A.T. in 1939 after its completion.

N-S	**Trail Description**	S-N

0.0   **Lehigh Gap** West end of the Pa. Rt. 873 highway   13.3
bridge across the Lehigh River.

Southbound Hikers: Turn right leaving the highway, passing a private driveway on the right. After passing the directional signs, turn right and proceed up the hillside following a gentle switchback. Cross open rocky area. Watch for blazes.

Northbound Hikers: To continue on A.T., cross Lehigh River on bridge.

0.2   Pass under power lines with fine views of Lehigh Gap.   13.1
Woods edge.

0.6   Reach the **George W. Outerbridge Shelter**.   12.7

0.7   Blue-blazed trail to the west, the North Trail, goes to   12.6
the top of the mountain and rejoins the A.T. at 2.3/11.1 mi. The North Trail is more scenic, but is open to winter storms. It passes another blue-blazed side trail in 0.3 mi. from its northern end and 2.0 mi from its southern end, which drops steeply 0.4 mi. to Devil's Pulpit with good views of the Lehigh Gap.

2.3   Southern junction of the A.T. and the North Trail. The   11.1
trail passes over the Northeast Extension of the Pennsylvania Turnpike, which goes through the mountain.

2.9   Northern junction of the A.T. and blue-blazed South   10.5
Trail. Trail rejoins A.T. at 4.0/9.4 mi.

4.0   Southern junction of the A.T. and blue-blazed South   9.4
Trail; the South Trail parallels the A.T. for 1.1 mi. and traverses rocky outcroppings offering good views. Footing requires extreme caution.

LEHIGH FURNACE GAP →

Ashfield Road is a cross-mountain road passable by auto in Lehigh Furnace Gap between Lehigh Furnace and Ashfield. Parking is available under transmission lines. To the east, along the road 0.7 mi. is a spring.

BAKE OVEN KNOB SHELTER →

Bake Oven Knob Shelter is one of the original shelters built in the 1930's. It is small with no privy. A campsite is on south side just below the A.T. A blue-blazed trail from the shelter leads down hill past an often dry spring on right and then to a second spring on the right in another 200 yards, and yet further to a third spring (near quarry which is on private property). All three springs are unreliable in dry weather. This trail continues to Bake Oven Knob Road and then to a paved road in the valley in 2.0 mi.

BAKE OVEN KNOB →

Bake Oven Knob is an internationally important and popular hawk migration observation site, especially in the fall. To the east is an exceptional lookout with 180 degree views compass south. To the west is a view compass north.

BAKE OVEN KNOB ROAD →

Bake Oven Knob Road is between Germansville and Andreas. A State Game Lands parking lot is available.

NEW TRIPOLI CAMPSITE →

A blue-blazed trail to the west descends 0.2 mi. to New Tripoli Campsite and spring.

N-S	**Trail Description**	S-N
5.0	Cross Ashfield Road in **Lehigh Furnace Gap**.	8.3
5.4	Southbound Hikers: Trail turns right, leaving woods road.	7.9
6.6	Rock outcrop gives winter views to the north.	6.7
7.4	**Bake Oven Knob Shelter**.	5.9
7.9	Base of steep rocky slide of knob.	5.4
8.0	**Bake Oven Knob**, elevation 1,560 ft., site of former air beacon.	5.3
	Northbound Hikers: Reach rockslide on north side of mountain. Cross slide using care.	
8.4	Cross State Game Lands parking lot and **Bake Oven Knob Road**, passable by auto.	4.9
8.8	Southbound Hikers: Turn left where road forks.	4.5
	Northbound Hikers: Bear right on fork at grassy road.	
9.8	Blue-blazed trail to the west climbs with difficulty to Bear Rocks with fine 360-degree views. Don't miss it but be careful on the rocks.	3.5
10.5	Cross the knife edge rocks known as "The Cliffs" with a view to the south.	2.9
11.5	A blue-blazed trail to the west descends 0.2 mi. to **New Tripoli Campsite** and spring. Cross under power line south of blue-blazed trail.	1.8

BLUE MOUNTAIN SUMMIT ➔

At Pa. Rt. 309 there is a State Game Lands parking lot just north of the Trail on the east side of the highway.

A.T. along ridge near Lehigh Gap © David Scheid

N-S <u>**Trail Description**</u> **S-N**

13.3   Pa. Rt. 309 at **Blue Mountain Summit,** elevation 1,360   0.0
ft. Blue-blazed trail on west, 130 ft. on the north side
of the highway crossing leads to parking area.

Southbound Hikers: To continue, cross Pa. Rt. 309
then descend on steps. Continue on footpath, turning
right in 50 yds.

George W. Outerbridge Shelter © Lorrie Preston

SECTION 4

PA. RT. 309 TO PORT CLINTON

DISTANCE: 26.7 Mi.

This section of the Trail is maintained by the Allentown Hiking Club from Pa. Rt. 309 to Tri-County Corner and by the Blue Mountain Eagle Climbing Club from Tri-County Corner to Port Clinton.

OVERVIEW OF SECTION 4

From Blue Mountain Summit at Pa. Rt. 309, the Trail stays on the ridge, with slight climbs to the Allentown Shelter and at Tri-County Corner. Then a rather sharp descent leads to Eckville. Leaving Eckville, the Trail climbs gradually and then steeply before leveling out on the ridge leading to the spectacular Pinnacle. A drop again into Windsor Furnace, and another climb precede the steep descent into Port Clinton. Points of interest along the way are Tri-County Corner, Dan's Pulpit, The Pinnacle, Pulpit Rock, Windsor Furnace and numerous charcoal hearths, such as the one at Pocahontas Spring. These hearths supplied fuel for the furnace. A special point of interest is the Hawk Mountain Sanctuary near Eckville. This is a world-renowned wildlife refuge and the first sanctuary in the world to offer protection to birds of prey.

GENERAL INFORMATION

MAPS

Use KTA Sections 1-6 Map. This section of trail is on the following USGS 7 1/2' quads: New Tripoli, New Ringgold, Hamburg, and Auburn.

SHELTERS AND DESIGNATED CAMPSITES

4.1 mi.   from Blue Mountain Summit is the Allentown Hiking Club Shelter. A spring is nearby.

11.5 mi. from Blue Mountain summit is the Eckville Shelter (0.2 mi. south on the road). In season has a flush toilet and shower with caretaker present. Water is also available from a faucet at the side of the caretaker's house when the caretaker is present.

20.6 mi. from Blue Mountain Summit is the Windsor Furnace Shelter. A spring and privy are nearby. Limited camping is permitted around the shelter.

PUBLIC ACCOMMODATIONS

Overnight or weekend lodging is available for hikers at the Y.W.C.A. Blue Mountain Camp, Hamburg, Pa. <u>DONATION REQUESTED</u>. Meals are available during the camp season, usually June 9 through the end of August. At other times of the year, prior arrangement must be made with the camp caretaker by calling 610-378-4700 or writing to Camp Director, YWCA, 8th & Washington Sts., Reading, Pa. 19601. The camp is one mile south of the A.T. on a blue-blazed side trail from Pocahontas Spring.

The Port Clinton Hotel, 0.5 mi. north of the Trail on Pa. Rt. 61, provides lodging for hikers. Accommodations and restaurants are available one mile south of Port Clinton at I-78 and in Hamburg, Pa., three miles south of Port Clinton on Pa. Rt. 61.

Port Clinton allows hikers to camp for free under the roof of its pavilion located 0.4 mi. north on Penn Street. Hikers must check in at the Ye Olde Backpacker or sign register. The pavilion is a drug- and alcohol-free area. Permission is required to stay more than two nights. Please be considerate and follow the town's rules for use of the pavilion or this privilege will disappear from the hiking community.

Blue Rocks Campground (1.5 mi. down yellow-blazed trail at 18.5 mi. from Blue Mountain Summit; 9.9 mi. from Port Clinton) offers camping, hot showers, laundry facilities, and a camp store.

SUPPLIES

Supplies can be purchased in Hamburg, Pa. There are no grocery stores in either Eckville or Port Clinton.

The Peanut Shop provides snacks. In Shartlesville (3.6 mi. one way) there are several famous eating places serving family style meals.

BLUE MOUNTAIN SUMMIT →

At Pa. Rt. 309 there is a State Game Lands parking lot just north of the Trail on the east side of the highway.

FORT FRANKLIN ROAD ←

This is a rough stone mountain road, which is passable by auto. A small parking lot is available.

ALLENTOWN SHELTER →

The privy is 200 feet west of the shelter. This blue-blazed trail leads another 1,200 feet to a spring, and then turns left connecting with the A.T. in an additional 375 ft. The spring may be dry by mid-summer, but water can always be found by following the yellow-blazed trail 1,100 feet down the south side of the mountain to a spring.

N-S	**Trail Description**	S-N

0.0	Pa. Rt. 309 at **Blue Mountain Summit**, elevation 1,360 ft. Blue-blazed trail on west, 130 ft. on the north side of the highway crossing leads to parking area. Southbound Hikers: Cross road, descend on steps and continue on footpath turning right in 50 yards.	26.7
0.4	Southbound Hikers: Trail turns left leaving footpath and continues on a State Game Lands road. Northbound Hikers: Bear right onto footpath.	26.3
1.8	Southbound Hikers: Bear left off State Game Lands road, Trail becomes a footpath. Northbound Hikers: Footpath ends, Trail turns right onto State Game Lands road.	24.9
2.2	Cross **Fort Franklin road**, passable by auto.	24.5
3.8	Blue-blazed trail leads to a spring in 375 feet, and leads to the Allentown Shelter. Southbound Hikers: A.T. turns sharp right up eroded woods road.	22.9
4.1	Blue-blazed trail to east leads 30 yards to the **Allentown Shelter.**	22.6
4.3	Southbound Hikers: Turn left off woods road. Trail becomes rocky. Northbound Hikers: Turn right onto woods road.	22.5

TRI-COUNTY CORNER ➜

Tri-County Corner is the place where, in 1926, a work party from the Blue Mountain Eagle Climbing Club first began construction on the Appalachian Trail in Pennsylvania.

DAN'S PULPIT ➜

Dan's Pulpit, named in honor of hiking's grand old man, Daniel K. Hoch, one of the founders of the Blue Mountain Eagle Climbing Club, who conducted Sunday services here. Excellent views of the Pinnacle and surrounding countryside.

N-S	**Trail Description**	S-N

5.3	A blue-blazed trail leads east, down the Old Dresher Road, not passable for autos and is closed near bottom of mountain by landowner.	21.4
	Southbound Hikers: The A.T. turns right upgrade on the Old Dresher Road.	
	Northbound Hikers: A.T. turns left. Trail becomes very rocky.	
5.4	**Tri-County Corner**. A blue-blazed trail to the west leads 400 ft. to the top of the rock pile where a marker indicates the intersection of Berks, Lehigh, and Schuylkill Counties.	21.3
5.5	Edge of woods road.	21.2
6.4	Balanced Rock on east.	20.3
7.4	Blue-blazed trail to the east leads steeply downhill 115 yards to Dan's Spring, not dependable.	19.4
8.0	Blue-blazed trail to east leads 1.9 mi. into the valley, passing a spring at 0.75 mi.	18.8
8.6	A few feet to the east of the Trail is **Dan's Pulpit**.	18.1
9.2	Southbound Hikers: Turn left on old woods road.	17.5
	Northbound Hikers: Leave old mountain road and turn right on foot trail.	

HAWK MOUNTAIN SANCTUARY →

It is the first sanctuary of its kind for protection of birds of prey. The vistas are spectacular, especially in the autumn during the hawk migration. Early September brings the American Bald Eagle followed by the great Broad-Winged Hawk migration in mid-September. Broadwings can be seen in large "kettles," sometimes numbering the hundreds that spiral above the outlooks. October offers the largest variety of hawks as well as the southward movements of waterfowl and the peak of autumn color. Visitors in late November stand a chance, especially on days with strong northwest winds, of seeing the majestic Golden Eagle.

A description of Hawk Mountain Sanctuary occurs in the beginning of the guide. No camping, fires, or pets are allowed on Sanctuary property or along the clearly-marked Hawk Mountain/A.T. Corridor.

HAWK MOUNTAIN ROAD →

The Trail crosses Hawk Mountain Road between the villages of Kempton, on Pa. Rt. 143, and Drehersville, on Pa. Rt. 895. This road is the access road to Hawk Mountain Sanctuary. Parking is available at a State Game Lands parking lot on the right side of southbound unimproved Pine Swamp Road, 0.5 mi. from Eckville, and 0.43 mi. from the A.T. on a blue-blazed trail.

ECKVILLE SHELTER →

The Eckville Shelter has flush toilet and shower with caretaker present in season. Water is also available from a faucet at the side of the caretaker's house when the caretaker is present.

N-S   <u>**Trail Description**</u>   **S-N**

9.7   A blue-blazed trail to the west leads two mi. to **Hawk**   17.0
        Mountain Sanctuary's North Lookout, and then to the
        headquarters and museum. A fee is charged to hike in
        the sanctuary. NO CAMPING IS PERMITTED.

        Southbound Hikers: A.T. turns sharp left down the
        mountain on an old road.

10.0   Southbound Hikers: Turn right off old road onto   16.7
        footpath.

        Northbound Hikers: Turn left onto abandoned cross-
        mountain road, climbing to the ridge.

11.2   Southbound Hikers: Turn right, then left, and come to   15.6
        log walkway and bridge over swamp and creek. Bear
        left, then sharp right.

        Northbound Hikers: Turn left off road, then sharp right.
        Come to bridge and walkway over creek and swamp.
        After swamp, turn right, then left.

11.3   Southbound Hikers: Turn right on old logging road.   15.4

        Northbound Hikers: Turn left on old logging road.

11.5   Cross **Hawk Mountain Road**. West leads to Hawk   15.2
        Mountain Sanctuary; East to Eckville and **Eckville**
        Shelter in 0.2 mi. by following blue blazes along road to
        shelter.

11.7   Southbound Hikers: Crossing of woods roads. Turn   14.4
        left.

View of Pinnacle from Pulpit Rock © Jeff Mitchell

PINNACLE →

At an elevation of 1,635 ft, the Pinnacle is considered by many to be the most spectacular vista along the A.T. in Pennsylvania. There are two caves below the Pinnacle, and many sheer cliffs to explore. There is a trail register on tree at the vista. NO CAMPING OR FIRES ALLOWED.

N-S	**Trail Description**	S-N

12.4 Southbound Hikers: Bear right off woods road onto State Game Lands service road. Old A.T. is now a 0.43 mi. blue-blazed trail to State Game Lands parking lot. 14.3

Northbound Hikers: Bear left off road. Old A.T. is now a 0.43 mi. blue-blazed trail to the State Game Lands parking lot.

13.3 Unmarked Panther Spring, always flowing, on west. 13.4

13.6 Southbound Hikers: A.T. turns left up the mountain on woods road. *EXCEPT AS NOTED IN THIS GUIDE, NO CAMPING OR FIRES ARE ALLOWED IN THIS AREA WHICH IS THE HAMBURG BOROUGH WATERSHED.* 13.1

14.2 Blue-blazed woods road on west leads to the A.T. at Windsor Furnace in 1.5 mi. 12.5

14.8 Reliable Gold Spring 30 yds on west. NO CAMPING OR FIRES. 11.9

15.1 Blue-blazed woods road goes west to Furnace Creek. 11.6

16.8 Blue-blazed trail to the east leads 80 yards to the spectacular **Pinnacle**. NO CAMPING OR FIRES. 9.9

17.2 Yellow-blazed trail to the east leads down a steep hill for 1.3 mi. to Blue Rocks. In another 0.2 mi. is the Blue Rocks Campground, privately owned, where supplies can be purchased at the camp store. 9.5

18.4 Pass through cleft in rock formation. 8.4

18.5 Rock field 10 yds to the west. 8.3

18.8 Excellent view to the west on a rock outcropping. Pass tower. 7.9

PULPIT ROCK →

Pulpit Rock on the east at 1,582 ft. elevation, with excellent views of the Pinnacle to the left and Blue Rocks in the foreground. NO CAMPING OR FIRES ALLOWED.

WINDSOR FURNACE SHELTER →

Limited camping permitted around the shelter.

WINDSOR FURNACE →

Arrive at trail sign and Windsor Furnace, site of an early pig iron works. Iron stoves were a specialty. Note glassy slag in the footpath. The remains of the old engine foundation are in the undergrowth. An essential ingredient was charcoal, and the Trail passes many flat round charcoal hearths, or burning sites, 30 to 50 ft. in diameter.

Mountain laurel along Trail © Wayne E. Gross

N-S	**Trail Description**	S-N
19.0	**Pulpit Rock** on the east. NO CAMPING OR FIRES ALLOWED.	7.7
19.2	Southbound Hikers: Trail bears left descending mountain on an old woods road.	7.5
19.5	Blue-blazed trail on east leads to Blue Rocks Campground.	7.2
20.6	Trail to the west leads 500 ft. to the **Windsor Furnace Shelter**.	6.2
20.7	Cross Furnace Creek. NO SWIMMING OR BATHING PERMITTED.	6.0
20.8	Edge of Hamburg Borough Watershed.	5.9

Arrive at trail sign and **Windsor Furnace**.

NO OTHER CAMPING IS ALLOWED.

Southbound Hikers: The A.T. turns left on an old woods road.

Northbound Hikers: A.T. is straight ahead.

NO CAMPING OR FIRES ARE ALLOWED IN THIS AREA WHICH IS THE HAMBURG BOROUGH WATERSHED. NO SWIMMING IS PERMITTED IN THE CREEK OR IN THE IMPOUNDMENT.

21.4	Southbound Hikers: Take right fork from woods road. Use care.	5.3
21.6	Intermittent stream, dry in summer.	5.1
22.2	Minnehaha spring, frequently dry.	4.5

PORT CLINTON ➔

Hikers can stay and eat at the Port Clinton Hotel. Packages can be mailed at the post office (ZIP Code 19549). There is a pavilion with water and pit toilet which hikers may use. Follow blue blazes for 0.4 mi. on Penn Street See information at beginning of section.

Parking on Port Clinton streets is limited. A ten-car parking area is located just south of Port Clinton along Pa. Rt. 61. It is accessible only from the southbound lane. It connects to the A.T. via a blue-blazed trail.

The town of Port Clinton developed around the canal system and is named after Governor DeWitt Clinton of Erie Canal fame. There is a Canal Museum in town.

N-S	**Trail Description**	S-N
23.4	Pocahontas Spring is usually reliable. A blue-blazed trail to the left leads one mi. to the YWCA Blue Mountain Camp.	3.3
24.3	Cross clearing for former telephone line.	2.5
24.4	Cross State Game Lands boundary line.	2.4
25.3	Top of ridge.	1.4
25.9	Road crossing and parking area. Base of mountain.	0.8
26.0	Southbound Hikers: Turn right under Pa. Rt. 61 highway bridge. Bear right along Schuylkill River.	0.7
	Northbound Hikers: Bear left and cross under Pa. Rt. 61.	
26.4	Blue-blazed trail on west leads 100 yds to parking area.	0.3
	Southbound Hikers: Turn right away from the river.	
	Northbound Hikers: Turn left.	
26.5	Southbound Hikers: Turn left on Broad St. and cross Little Schuylkill River.	0.2
	Northbound Hikers: Turn right on Penn St. and then bear right into woods along Schuylkill River.	
26.7	Cross Schuylkill River on railroad bridge in **Port Clinton**.	0.0

SECTION 5

PORT CLINTON TO PA. RT. 183

DISTANCE: 14.4 Mi.

This section of the Trail is maintained by the Blue Mountain Eagle Climbing Club.

OVERVIEW OF SECTION 5

The Trail begins with a steep climb out of Port Clinton, gaining 1,000 feet in two miles. The footway is quite rocky for most of the first six miles. Beyond, the Trail passes through a maturing forest that is surprisingly rock-free, and altogether pleasant hiking. The State Game Lands Road, over which the Trail was previously routed, is crossed five times before reaching Pa. Rt. 183.

GENERAL INFORMATION

MAPS
Use KTA Sections 1-6 Map. This section of trail is on the following USGS 7 1/2' quads: Auburn and Friedensburg

SHELTERS AND DESIGNATED CAMPSITES

8.6 mi.   from Port Clinton is Eagles Nest Shelter for eight. Yeich
            Spring is nearby.

Camping is permitted in this section since almost all of the Trail is in
State Game Lands, but PA Game Commission camping regulations as
outlined on page 57 must be followed.

PUBLIC ACCOMMODATIONS

Overnight or weekend lodging is available for hikers at the Y.W.C.A.
Blue Mountain Camp, Hamburg, Pa. <u>DONATION REQUESTED</u>.
Meals are available during the camp season, usually June 9 through
the end of August. At other times of the year, prior arrangement must
be made with the camp caretaker by calling 610-378-4700 or writing
to Camp Director, YWCA, 8th & Washington Sts., Reading, Pa.
19601. The camp is one mile south of the A.T. on a blue-blazed side
trail from Pocahontas Spring.

The Port Clinton Hotel, 0.5 mi. north of the Trail on Pa. Rt. 61,
provides lodging for hikers. Accommodations and restaurants are
available one mile south of Port Clinton at I-78 and in Hamburg, Pa.,
three miles south of Port Clinton on Pa. Rt. 61.

Port Clinton allows hikers to camp for free under the roof of its
pavilion located 0.4 mi. north on Penn Street. Hikers must check in at
the Ye Olde Backpacker or sign register. The pavilion is a drug- and
alcohol-free area. Permission is required to stay more than two
nights. Please be considerate and follow the town's rules on use of
the pavilion or this privilege will disappear from the hiking
community.

Blue Rocks Campground (1.5 mi. down yellow-blazed trail at 18.5 mi.
from Blue Mountain Summit; 9.9 mi. from Port Clinton) offers
camping, hot showers, laundry facilities, and a camp store.

The Peanut Shop provides snacks. In Shartlesville (3.6 mi. one way)
there are several famous eating places serving family style meals. In
Hamburg there are hotels and motels.

SUPPLIES

There are grocery stores in Hamburg, three miles south of Port Clinton. There are no groceries in Shartlesville.

In Port Clinton there is an outfitter, Ye Olde Backpacker.

PORT CLINTON ➜

Hikers can stay and eat at the Port Clinton Hotel. Packages can be mailed at the post office (ZIP Code 19549). There is a pavilion with water and pit toilet which hikers may use. Follow blue blazes for 0.4 mi. on Penn Street.

Parking on Port Clinton streets is limited. A ten-car parking area is located just south of Port Clinton along Pa. Rt. 61. It is accessible only from the southbound lane. It connects to the A.T. via a blue-blazed trail.

The town of Port Clinton developed around the canal system and is named after Governor DeWitt Clinton of Erie Canal fame. There is a Canal Museum in town.

AUBURN LOOKOUT ➜

Excellent view of Auburn village and surrounding area from Auburn Lookout.

N-S	**Trail Description**	S-N

0.0   **Port Clinton**, PA and Pa. Rt. 61   14.4

Southbound Hikers: Cross the Schuylkill River on the railroad/road bridge. Turn left onto railroad/road and turn right across tracks.

Northbound Hikers: Reach railroad bridge over Schuylkill River and end of section. Turn right on Broad St. in Port Clinton. Parking is limited in the borough; use area on side road east of Pa. Rt. 61, 0.5 mi. south of the Borough.

0.1   Southbound Hikers: Climb steep bank to old single railroad bed. Continue left on track for 175 ft. Turn right uphill ascending very steeply for the next 0.5 mi.   14.3

Northbound Hikers: Come to old railroad bed. Turn left for 175 ft. then descend bank on right via path to railroad tracks. Cross tracks to paved driveway.

1.0   Cross pipeline.   13.4

1.4   Cross pipeline.   10.0

1.5   A.T. makes sharp turn.   12.9

2.0   Cross State Game Lands road.   12.2

2.4   Come to State Game Lands road. Follow road to the right (but do not cross) for about 45 yds and re-enter woods.   12.0

2.5   Reach **Auburn Lookout**, a rock outcrop off the Trail to the east.   11.9

3.1   Cross blue-blazed Marshalls Path.   11.3

EAGLES NEST SHELTER →

Eagles Nest Shelter has room for eight people. Water available from Yeich Spring 0.1 mi. away. Composting privy is provided.

N-S	**Trail Description**	S-N
3.3	State Game Lands road. Cross diagonally, following arrows, cairns, and blazes for about 120 yds. Enter woods on trail that is now south of the road.	11.1
4.0	Pass unmarked Phillip's Canyon Spring trail on the east. Spring is 135 yds down a steep descent and is unreliable. Spring is at a stone enclosure.	10.4
5.2	State Game Lands road. Cross directly, following arrows, cairns and blazes for about 100 yds. Trail enters woods.	9.2
5.7	Sharp turn.	8.7
6.1	A.T. turns.	8.3
6.7	Cross old mountain road. To the east is a State Game Lands parking lot, 1.6 mi., and Shartlesville, 3.6 mi.	7.7
8.6	Come to blue-blazed trail that leads in 0.2 mi. to intermittent Yeich Spring, 0.3 mi. to **Eagles Nest Shelter**, and 0.4 mi. to vista. Cross State Game Lands-Weiser State Forest boundary.	5.8
8.8	Cross State Game Lands road.	5.6
9.3	Cross blue-blazed Sand Spring Trail. Sand Spring, a fine walled spring is located 0.14 mi. to the east. NO CAMPING is permitted at or near the spring.	5.1
12.0	Cross small stream.	2.4
13.1	Blue-blazed trail to east leads 300 yds. to unreliable Black Swatara Spring. NO CAMPING.	1.3
13.9	Cross State Game Lands road. State Game Lands parking lot is to the east at the foot of this road and adjacent to Pa. Rt. 183.	0.5

PA RT 183 →

The Trail crosses Pa. Rt. 183 between Strausstown and Summit Station. The Pa. Rt. 183 crossing is a dangerous, four lane, high speed, well traveled crossing with limited sight distance for hikers. Cross with care. There is a State Game Lands parking lot 0.3 mi. south of the mountaintop on the east side of the road.

RENTSCHLER MARKER →

Dr. H. F. Rentschler led the work parties which, beginning in 1926, originally established the A.T. between the Lehigh and Susquehanna Rivers.

N-S	**Trail Description**	S-N

14.0   Southbound Hikers: Turn left onto woods road.   0.4

Northbound Hikers: Leave woods road, turning right onto trail.

14.4   Southbound Hikers: Pass **Rentschler Marker**, 15 yds   0.0
to the right. Reach **Pa. Rt. 183**.

Northbound Hikers: Trail crosses **Pa. Rt. 183** at official PennDOT highway sign marking the A.T. Trail follows road up slight incline and immediately passes **Rentschler Marker**, 15 yds off to the left. Trail continues on woods road.

SECTION 6

PA. RT. 183 TO SWATARA GAP

DISTANCE: 20.7 Mi.

This section of the Trail is maintained by the Blue Mountain Eagle Climbing Club.

OVERVIEW OF SECTION 6

Except for a slight dip in Shuberts Gap, the Trail stays on the ridge until the final descent into Swatara Gap. Points of interest along the way are the site of Fort Dietrich Snyder (1756), one of a chain of forts and blockhouses built as protection from the Indians; Showers Steps, 500 rough stone steps forming a path down the point of Round Head, built by Lloyd Showers; and Pilger Ruh Spring, a colonial watering stop.

GENERAL INFORMATION

MAPS

Use KTA Sections 1-6 Map. This section of trail is on the following USGS 7 1/2' quads: Friedensburg, Swatara Hill, Pine Grove, Fredericksburg, Indiantown Gap.

SHELTERS AND DESIGNATED CAMPSITES

3.7 mi.   Hertlein Campsite is located in Shuberts Gap. Streams are nearby.

8.8 mi.   Applebee Campsite is located near Pilger Ruh (Pilgrims Rest) Spring.

9.3 mi.   from Pa. Rt. 183 is the Rt. 501 Shelter: fully enclosed, water, port-a-potty (in season). There is a caretaker year-round.

13.4 mi.   from Pa. Rt. 183 is the William Penn Shelter, a two-story structure with two sleeping levels. The second level is a loft with windows.

PUBLIC ACCOMMODATIONS

Lodging and restaurants are available in Pine Grove, Pa..

The Bashore Boy Scout Reservation may be used by hiking groups if advance arrangements are made with the Camp Director, Camp Bashore, Pennsylvania Dutch Boy Scout Council Office, 630 Janet Ave. Suite B-116, Lancaster, Pa. 17601 www.padutchcouncil.org.

There is a motel and a privately owned campground in the village of Lickdale.

SUPPLIES

A store and restaurant is located 0.8 mi. south of A.T. in Swatara Gap along Pa. Rt. 72; hikers welcome. There are convenience stores and restaurants in the village of Lickdale 2.4 mi. south along Pa. Rt. 72. The village can be reached via a blue-blazed trail beginning at the Waterville Bridge.

At Pa. Rt. 501 crossing groceries can be obtained at stores in Pine Grove to the north and in Mt. Bethel to the south.

PA. RT. 183 →

The Trail crosses. Rt. 183 between Strausstown and Summit Station. The Pa. Rt. 183 crossing is a dangerous, four lane, high speed, well traveled crossing with limited sight distance for hikers. Cross with care. There is a State Game Lands parking lot 0.3 mi. south of the mountaintop on the east side of the road.

RENTSCHLER MARKER →

Dr. H. F. Rentschler led the work parties which, beginning in 1926, originally established the A.T. between the Lehigh and Susquehanna Rivers.

FORT DIETRICH SNYDER →

A marker indicates the site of Fort Dietrich Snyder (1756), one of a chain of forts erected along the Blue Mountain as protection against Indian Raids during the French and Indian War. Col. Benjamin Franklin at one time commanded this fort. (See chapter on history.)

HERTLEIN CAMPSITE →

Hertlein Campsite is located in Shuberts Gap. Two tent platforms are located here. A blue-blazed trail to the east leads downhill to a dam and pond. Below the dam is private property; do not trespass.

ROUND HEAD AND SHOWERS STEPS →

Round Head has a great view. Lloyd Showers, an early Trail worker, constructed a path of 500 rough stone steps down the face of Round Head. A blue-blazed path continues through the Kessel (Kettle) which is now closed by land owner. At the base of Showers Steps is a spring. South on the A.T. in 200 feet is the Shanaman Marker.

William F. Shanaman was Mayor of Reading, Pa. and an early Trail worker.

N-S	**Trail Description**	S-N

0.0   **Pa. Rt. 183** north of Stausstown and south of Summit   20.7
Station.

Southbound Hikers: At the official Pennsylvania Department of Transportation signboard, cross the highway to the west side; go up a slight bank and follow signs and blazes across a large open field on an old road leading to the former Shuberts Summit cross-mountain road.

Northbound Hikers: Trail crosses Pa. Rt. 183 at official Pennsylvania Department of Transportation signboard marking the A.T. Trail follows road up slight incline and immediately passes **Rentschler marker**, 15 yds off to the left. Trail continues on woods road.

0.3   Reach historical marker for **Fort Dietrich Snyder**. A.T.   20.4
turns sharply at marker. Blue-blazed trail leads north to reliable Fort Dietrich Snyder Spring in 0.13 mi. which can be reached by going north on the cross-mountain road for 125 yards. Turn left across a clearing to reach spring in the woods.

2.9   Cross oil pipeline.   17.8

3.6   Arrive in Shuberts Gap.   17.1

3.7   **Hertlein Campsite**. Cross stream south of campsite.   17.0
A Trail register box is on a tree.

4.1   Reach Shikellamy Summit, a fine lookout.   16.6

5.2   Reach a charcoal hearth on west.   15.5

6.2   Reach **Round Head and Showers Steps** (blue-blazed   14.5
trail) and a great viewpoint.

PILGER RUH ➔

Pilger Ruh (Pilgrims Rest) Spring was a watering stop dating back to colonial times. Conrad Weiser and others stopped here on their travels to secure treaties with the Indians.

APPLEBEE CAMPSITE ➔

Applebee Campsite is located a short distance west of the junction of the A.T. and the blue-blazed trail to Pilger Ruh Spring.

PA. RT. 501 ➔

The AT can be accessed by Pa. Rt. 501 between Bethel and Pine Grove. There is parking just north of the crossing.

Rt. 501 SHELTER ➔

The shelter is 0.16 mi. on the blue-blazed trail on the north side Pa. Rt. 501.

KIMMEL LOOKOUT ➔

Kimmel Lookout, an outstanding viewpoint named for Richard Kimmel. He was a Trail worker for over 40 years, and an honorary member of ATC. He served many years as a Boy Scout leader and regularly led Sunday morning worship services at KTA weekends.

PA. RT. 645 ➔

The Trail crosses Pa. Rt. 645 between Frystown and Pine Grove. A parking lot is on the west side of the road.

WILLIAM PENN SHELTER ➔

William Penn Shelter includes a loft with windows and composting privy.

N-S	**Trail Description**	S-N
6.3	An unmarked trail to east leads 100 ft. to unnamed lookout. Great view of the Kessel and north to Second and Sharp Mountains.	14.4
6.8	A.T. turns.	13.9
7.4	Blue-blazed Kessel Trail on east is closed.	13.3
8.8	Blue-blazed trail to the east leads to **Pilger Ruh** (Pilgrims Rest) Spring, a watering stop dating back to colonial times. Camping is permitted at **Applebee Campsite**.	11.9
9.3	Reach **Pa. Rt. 501**. Watch for signs to **Rt. 501 Shelter**.	11.4
9.4	**Kimmel Lookout**	11.3
9.5	Cross buried cable line clearing.	11.2
11.2	Reach **Pa. Rt. 645** between Frystown and Pine Grove at site of radio tower.	9.5
13.4	Blue-blazed trail to the west leads to Blue Mountain Spring, 225 yards downhill. Blue-blazed trail to east leads 0.12 mi. to **William Penn Shelter**.	7.3
14.6	Cross oil pipeline. To the east in 200 yards is a tri-county marker denoting the intersection of Berks, Lebanon and Schuylkill Counties.	6.1
16.1	View over Monroe Valley is to the east.	4.6
17.4	Dip into hollow passing the old charcoal road leading downhill to the east into Monroe Valley.	3.3

Pilger Ruh © Thomas Scully

WATERVILLE BRIDGE ➔

The Waterville Bridge is a cast iron bridge built in 1890 across the Little Pine Creek in Lycoming County. The bridge design is a lenticular truss (parabolic) and is one of three such bridges still in Pennsylvania. After being determined to be too narrow for modern traffic patterns the bridge was dismantled and placed over the Swatara Creek in the 1980's.

PA. RT. 72 ➔

In Swatara Gap, Trail access is from Pa. Rt. 72, just south of the Interstate 81 overpass. There is no access from Interstate 81. Pa. Rt. 72 goes north from the village of Lickdale at the intersection where Pa. Rt. 72 turns. No designated parking.

The development of Swatara State Park is planned for this area. When construction begins, parking areas will be designated by signs. Parking may be arranged at the Bashore Boy Scout Reservation, 0.9 mi. west of the A.T. at intersection of Pa. Rt. 443 and Ridge Road, by advance permission of the Camp Director.

N-S	**Trail Description**	S-N
18.3	The white-blazed State Game Lands boundary and the A.T. run together at this point. Use caution.	2.4
19.3	Crest of mountain.	1.4
19.4	Cross circle of old charcoal hearth.	1.3
19.9	Cross woods road.	0.7
20.1	Fence along Interstate 81. Follow blazes along and near fence. Do not cross the fence. Look for spring.	0.6
20.3	Pass under I-81 bridges.	0.4
	Southbound Hikers: Turn right onto Old State Road along the Swatara Creek.	
	Northbound Hikers: Turn left, then right, onto hard-surfaced Old State Road along Swatara Creek	
20.6	Cross Swatara Creek on **Waterville Bridge**.	0.1
20.7	**Pa. Rt. 72.**	0.0

SECTION 7

SWATARA GAP TO CLARKS VALLEY

DISTANCE: 17.4 Mi.

This section of the Trail is maintained by the Blue Mountain Eagle Climbing Club from Swatara Gap to Rausch Gap Shelter side trail, and by the Susquehanna Appalachian Trail Club from Rausch Gap Shelter side trail to Pa. Rt. 325 in Clarks Valley.

OVERVIEW OF SECTION 7

Leaving Swatara State Park, the Trail crosses Second Mountain, then descends into Stony Creek Valley and enters St. Anthony's Wilderness, the largest roadless tract in southeastern Pennsylvania. Historic Rausch Gap Village is directly on the Trail. An exploration of the area will reveal building foundations, a cemetery, old hand dug wells, abandoned railroad beds, railroad facilities, and other remains of a once thriving industrial community. (See the chapter on history.) The Trail goes through Rausch Gap, and then gently ascends Sharp Mountain and Stony Mountain before dropping into Clarks Valley. In addition to Rausch Gap Village and Yellow Springs Village (a long abandoned coal mining community), a point of interest is the northern terminus of the Horse-Shoe Trail on top of Sharp Mountain. During times when the trees are not in leaf it is possible from Stony Mountain to see DeHart Reservoir, which is the Harrisburg water supply reservoir.

GENERAL INFORMATION

MAPS

Use KTA Sections 7 & 8 Map. This section of trail is on the following USGS 7 1/2' quads: Tower City, Indiantown Gap, Grantville, and Enders.

SHELTERS AND DESIGNATED CAMPSITES

6.1 mi.   from Swatara Gap, in Rausch Gap, the Rausch Gap Shelter has a reliable spring and an outhouse. This shelter was built in 1972 by the Blue Mountain Eagle Climbing Club with the permission of the PA Game Commission. No camping or fires are permitted except as authorized. This shelter is for the use of thru-hikers only. The area is patrolled by PA Game Commission Wildlife Conservation Officers, who enforce regulations. Ruins from the coal mining era can be found scattered through the woods near the shelter.

PUBLIC ACCOMMODATIONS

The Bashore Boy Scout Reservation may be used by hiking groups if advance arrangements are made with the Camp Director, Camp Bashore, Pennsylvania Dutch Boy Scout Council Office, 630 Janet Ave. Suite B-116, Lancaster, Pa. 17601 www.padutchcouncil.org.

There is a motel and a privately owned campground in the village of Lickdale.

SUPPLIES

A convenience store and restaurant is located 0.8 mi. south of A.T. in Swatara Gap along Pa. Rt. 72; hikers welcome. There are convenience stores and restaurants in the village of Lickdale 2.4 mi. south along Pa. Rt. 72. The village can be reached via a blue-blazed trail beginning at the Waterville Bridge.

PA. RT. 72 →

In Swatara Gap, Trail access is from Pa. Rt. 72, just north of the Interstate 81 overpass. There is no access from Interstate 81. Pa. Rt. 72 goes north from the village of Lickdale at the intersection where Pa. Rt. 72 turns. No designated parking.

The development of Swatara State Park is planned for this area. When construction begins parking areas will be designated by signs. Parking may be arranged at the Bashore Boy Scout Reservation, 0.9 mi. west of the A.T. at intersection of Pa. Rt. 443 and Ridge Road, by advance permission of the Camp Director.

PA. RT. 443 →

At Pa. Rt. 443 near Pa. Rt. 72, there is a small parking lot on state park property on the Trail.

RAUSCH GAP →

Rausch Gap was a busy mining and railroad town in the 1800's. There are various types of ruins throughout the abandoned village site. Some are barely visible.

Susquehanna and Schuylkill Railroad ceased operations in the 1940's and is now a State Game Lands service road and used as a multi use trail in State Game Lands No. 211. To compass east the multi use trail leads 3.6 mi. to Gold Mine Road and a State Game Lands parking lot. To compass west the multi use trail leads 2.5 mi. to the Cold Spring Trail and 14.0 mi. to Ellendale Forge and another State Game Lands parking lot. The Cold Spring Trail descends to a State Game Lands parking lot and a rough road that leads to Indiantown Gap.

RAUSCH GAP SHELTER →

Rausch Gap Shelter is built on original stone ruins. A spring and outhouse is nearby.

A trail leads west along Rausch Creek and past some interesting stone ruins. Hikers may use Haystack Creek as water source if Rausch Gap Shelter spring is dry. Rausch Creek is being treated for acid mine run off contamination.

N-S	**Trail Description**	S-N

0.0   **Pa. Rt. 72**   17.4

Southbound Hikers: From west side of Pa. Rt. 72 begin gradual uphill climb.

1.4   **Pa. Rt. 443** and small parking lot.   16.0

2.0   Cross Pa. Rt. 443, then Greenpoint Schoolhouse Road.   15.4

4.4   Saddle of Second Mountain. Several un-blazed trails intersect here.   13.0

5.2   Cross Haystack Creek on a wooden footbridge.   12.2

5.5   Reach the center of the ruins of **Rausch Gap** Village. Do not build fires or camp here per PA Game Commission regulations.   11.9

5.6   Reach the old railroad bed of the Susquehanna and Schuylkill Railroad, and is now a State Game Lands service road and multiuse trail. Cross Rausch Creek on the old stone-arch railroad bridge.   11.8

5.7   Southbound Hikers: Turn right and follow old mine road uphill.   11.7

Northbound Hikers: Trail turns left onto the multiuse service road. Use care in following blazes through old mining area. On the right the multiuse trail goes along the old railroad bed and leads 2.5 mi. to the Cold Spring Trail, which leads south from the multiuse trail to a State Game Lands parking lot.

6.1   Blue-blazed trail leads 0.2 mi. to **Rausch Gap Shelter** and spring.   11.3

ST. ANTHONY'S WILDERNESS →

Between Pa. Rt. 443 and Pa. Rt. 325, the Appalachian Trail passes through St. Anthony's Wilderness, unbroken by habitation for 14 mi. This land is now owned and managed by the Pennsylvania Game Commission.

Scattered through the area are a number of long abandoned coal mines which were in operation more than 100 years ago and were serviced by a branch of the Reading Railroad. The old rail bed, which now serves as a multiuse trail, follows Stony Creek for 15 mi. from Gold Mine Road in the east to Ellendale Forge in the west

The village of Rausch Gap, just off the A.T. near the Stony Creek Rail Trail, flourished about 1850. Today little remains but a dry stone well about 20 feet from the Trail. The village at one time was populous enough to support a Catholic mission, and there is a small cemetery 150 feet away containing three gravestones of the John Proud family. The stones are dated 1853. If others were buried here, no stones remain to indicate it.

The Appalachian Trail used to follow an old stage coach road for many miles through the Wilderness. Side trails lead down to the former sites of the railroad stations of Yellow Springs and Cold Springs.

In 1880 a syndicate of Harrisburg men built a summer hotel there at a time when mineral baths were very popular. Remains of some foundations still exist.

YELLOW SPRINGS VILLAGE →

The blue-blazed Yellow Springs Trail to the west leads 0.3 mi. to the site of a stone tower and an old mine entrance. From there it goes 0.1 mi. to a loading ramp area for the inclined plane and returns to the A.T. in 0.77 mi. The Stone Tower Trail can be descended to Pa. Rt. 325. The A.T. at the site of Yellow Springs Village continues straight through the village site. The Yellow Springs Trail to the east was severely damaged by storm runoff and is not recommended.

N-S	**Trail Description**	S-N

6.3   Pass old open-cut strip mine on east, with Rausch Creek   11.1
on west.

Southbound Hikers: The Trail now follows an old stage
road for the next 7.0 mi.

Northbound Hikers: Trail bears right, leaving the old
stage road. Pass a large open-cut strip mine on the
right, with Rausch Creek on the left.

8.5   Junction with Cold Spring Trail which leads compass   8.9
south downhill 0.7 mi. to the multi use trail and to a
State Game Lands parking area at 0.9 mi. The rough
road from this parking lot goes to Indiantown Gap

Southbound Hikers: Bear right at a small clearing and
continue on old stage road.

Northbound Hikers: A.T. bears left.

8.7   Junction with the blue-blazed Sand Spring Trail on   8.7
compass north, which leads up and over Stony
Mountain to Rt. 325 in 1.7 mi.. Water can be found at a
stream along the side trail in 0.16 mi.

10.7   Pass through the ruins of **Yellow Springs Village** in **St.**   6.7
Anthony's Wilderness.

10.9   Junction with blue-blazed Yellow Springs Trail in a   6.5
narrow ravine with seasonal water.

12.6   Southbound Hikers: Bear right. The unmaintained stage   4.8
road continues straight ahead, descending 0.9 mi. to the
ruins of Rattling Run village and intersects the Horse-
Shoe Trail and the multi use trail.

Northbound Hikers: A.T. turns left onto an old stage
road, which the Trail follows for 7.0 mi.

HORSE-SHOE TRAIL ➔

The Horse-Shoe Trail leads to Valley Forge, PA, a total of 140 mi. For more information about the Horse-Shoe Trail, contact the Horse-Shoe Trail Conservancy at www.hstrail.org.

CLARKS VALLEY ➔

The A.T. crosses Pa. Rt. 325 in Clarks Valley, where there is a large State Game Lands parking lot at Clark Creek. No camping allowed at this site; Wildlife Conservation Officers will issue fines. This Trail crossing is located 10.1 mi. east of the intersection of Pa. Rt. 325 and Pa. Rt. 225, 2.0 mi. north of the village of Dauphin.

N-S	**Trail Description**	S-N
13.5	Cross Rattling Run on stepping stones among rhododendron.	3.9
14.1	Reach the summit of Stony Mountain.	3.3
	Southbound Hikers: Follow old road for next 1.8 mi.	
14.2	This is the northern terminus of the **Horse-Shoe Trail**, marked by a monument stone.	3.2
14.7	Pass intermittent spring beside the Trail.	2.7
15.2	Pass intermittent spring beside the Trail.	2.2
15.7	Cross acid mine drainage discharge from old coal mine.	1.7
16.0	Southbound Hikers: The Trail veers left off of old road and onto a newer section of graded Trail through many rock boulders.	1.4
	Northbound Hikers: Follow old road.	
16.4	Cross intermittent stream on a stone slab bridge.	1.0
16.9	Red-blazed Henry Knauber Trail on east leads very steeply up the mountain and reaches the Horse-Shoe Trail in 1.6 mi.	0.5
17.0	Reliable spring on A.T.	0.4
17.3	Blue-blazed Water Tank Trail on east follows along an old service road.	0.1
17.4	Cross Pa. Rt. 325 in **Clarks Valley**.	0.0

SECTION 8

CLARKS VALLEY TO SUSQUEHANNA RIVER

DISTANCE: 16.7 Mi.

This section of the Trail is maintained from Pa. Rt. 325 to Pa. Rt. 225 by the Susquehanna Appalachian Trail Club and from Pa. Rt. 225 to the Susquehanna River by the York Hiking Club.

OVERVIEW OF SECTION 8

After the initial climb to the crest of Peters Mountain, on switchbacks, the Trail stays on the ridge top with only minor changes in elevation until the descent to the Susquehanna River. This descent is gradual, using switchbacks to reach the railroad and the Clarks Ferry Bridge.

Points of interest along the Trail include Kinter View, Table Rock Overlook, many large rock outcrops and excellent views up and down the Susquehanna River. The Juniata River can be seen to the north, and to the south is the Rockville Bridge, the longest stone arch railroad bridge in the world. This bridge, built in 1902, carries Norfolk Southern's mainline tracks across the Susquehanna River. It also carried the A.T. until 1955.

GENERAL INFORMATION

MAPS

Use KTA Sections 7 & 8 Map. This section of trail is on the following USGS 7 1/2' quads: Enders, Halifax, and Duncannon.

SHELTERS AND DESIGNATED CAMPSITES

6.7 mi.   from Clarks Valley is the Peters Mountain Shelter and privy. A spring is located 357 yds. down a steep stone stepped blue-blazed trail on the north side of the mountain. The shelter was constructed by SATC volunteers from 1993 to 1994.

13.4 mi.   from Clarks Valley is the Clarks Ferry Shelter. Good spring.

PUBLIC ACCOMMODATIONS

The town of Duncannon, through which the Trail passes, is 0.6 mi. south of this section. Duncannon offers lodging and restaurants.

SUPPLIES

There are no sources of supplies on this section of the Trail until west end of Clarks Ferry Bridge. Supplies may be purchased in Duncannon. A supermarket, post office, and other amenities are available.

CLARKS VALLEY ➔

The A.T. crosses Pa. Rt. 325 in Clarks Valley, where there is a large State Game Lands parking lot at Clark Creek. No camping allowed at this site. Wildlife Conservation Officers will issue fines. This trail crossing is located 10.1 mi. east of the intersection of Pa. Rt. 325 and Pa. Rt. 225, 2.0 mi. north of the village of Dauphin.

IBBERSON CONSERVATION AREA ➔

After he graduated from Yale University in 1948, Joseph E. Ibberson went to work for the Commonwealth of Pennsylvania. He developed some of the forestry management plans for the 2,000,000 acres of state forests. Ibberson also helped to create the many divisions within what is now the Pennsylvania Department of Conservation and Natural Resources. He donated this 370 acre tract of land on December 9, 1998 to DCNR. This became the first conservation area in the Pennsylvania Bureau of State Parks.

PETERS MOUNTAIN SHELTER ➔

Water is found at a spring located 0.2 mi. down a very steep stone step blue-blazed trail on the north side of the mountain, which includes over 270 stone steps. This large shelter has a loft and a privy that were finished in 1994.

N-S	**Trail Description**	S-N
0.0	Cross Pa. Rt. 325 in **Clarks Valley**.	16.7
	Southbound Hikers: Enter the woods in State Game Lands No. 211 and begin ascent of Peters Mountain.	
0.3	Blue-blazed trail leads 136 yds to a reliable spring.	16.4
2.6	Blue-blazed Shikellimy Trail to the east leads down the mountain 0.9 mi. to Pa. Rt. 325 and roadside parking.	14.1
3.3	Shikellimy Rocks with winter views overlooking Clarks Valley.	13.4
4.0	Blue-blazed trail to the east leads to Kinter View at a small cliff in 60 yds with good views of Clarks Valley.	12.7
5.1	Junction with pink-blazed Whitetail Trail, a cross-mountain trail, which is part of the trail network of the **Ibberson Conservation Area.**	11.6
5.7	Intersection with blue-blazed Victoria Trail on east which continues 0.6 mi. to Pa. Rt. 325 and a State Game Lands parking lot. Limited view 100 feet from A.T. On the west the blue-blazed Victoria Trail leads 1.2 mi. to day use parking area in Ibberson Conservation Area.	11.0
6.7	Reach the **Peters Mountain Shelter**.	10.0
7.4	Yellow-blazed private trail to west leads in 1.5 mi. to Camp Hebron, a church camp. Use of camp trails is by permission only; a fee is charged.	9.3
7.5	Table Rock is 33 yards to east on blue-blazed trail with a good view to the south.	9.2

PA. RT. 225 ◄

The A.T. crosses Pa. Rt. 225 at the crest of Peters Mountain on pedestrian bridge. Entrance to the lot is on south side of ridge crest and on east side of highway about 200 feet below crest. The parking lot is out of sight from highway. Take paved driveway uphill approximately 200 feet to parking lot on left. An information bulletin board is at the parking lot. The pedestrian bridge over the highway is accessed from the parking area.

CLARKS FERRY SHELTER ◄

A blue-blazed side trail to east leads 300 ft. to the Clarks Ferry Shelter and 600 ft. to a reliable piped spring.

N-S	**Trail Description**	S-N

8.9   Pass under double power lines with excellent views to the north. Views south are possible if you climb the rock on the crest.   7.8

9.3   View south toward Harrisburg and Dauphin Narrows.   7.4

9.5   Footbridge over **Pa. Rt. 225**. Parking area with information bulletin board on north side of bridge. View north from the bridge.   7.2

12.2   Cross pipeline with good views south to Dauphin Gap, Rockville Railroad Bridge, and Harrisburg.   4.5

12.4   Pass a rock overhang that could be used as an emergency shelter.   4.3

13.1   Cross under the power line. From the crest there are excellent views of the Rockville Bridge to the south and the Juniata and Susquehanna Rivers to the north.   3.6

Southbound Hikers: After leaving the power line clearing, continue along the ridge top before descending onto a level area on the south face of the mountain.

Northbound Hikers: The Trail follows an old woods road for about 400 yds.

13.4   Blue-blazed side trail to east leads 300 ft. to the **Clarks Ferry Shelter**, and 600 ft. to a reliable piped spring.   3.3

13.7   Crest of the mountain, with blue-blazed Susquehanna Trail that rejoins the Trail 2 mi. south along A.T. The blue-blazed trail is 1.0 mi. long.   3.0

CLARKS FERRY BRIDGE

At the west end of the Clarks Ferry Bridge along U.S. Rts. 22 & 32
parking is limited. On the east end of the bridge is adequate parki
along the river, adjacent to the highway that is heavily used. Parking
also available on the streets of Duncannon. An information bulletin boa
is at the base of the mountain next to the railroad tracks.

N-S	**Trail Description**	S-N

14.7   Point of mountain.   2.0

Southbound   Hikers: Begin   descent   via   large
switchbacks.

Northbound Hikers: The Trail follows the crest to the
east through wooded areas and over rock outcroppings
that offer good views to the north and south.

15.2   View of Sherman's Creek and town of Duncannon   1.5
across the Susquehanna River.

15.3   Logging road.   1.4

Southbound Hikers: Follow road a short distance; turn
left and descend a short distance before turning right.
After a short distance, cross an intermittent stream.

Northbound Hikers: Turn right and follow the road to
the end.   The Trail continues up to the top of the
mountain.

15.4   Old stone foundation for a mule barn that was part of   1.3
the Berkeheimer Farm, which burned between 1910
and 1920.

15.7   Junction with blue-blazed Susquehanna Trail that   1.0
rejoins the Trail 2 mi. north along A.T.

16.7   West end of the **Clarks Ferry Bridge** across the   0.0
Susquehanna River.

Northbound Hikers: Cross the bridge on the pedestrian
walkway. At the compass east end of the bridge cross
the highway with care.   Turn left at the A.T. sign.
Walk 100 yds along the road.

SECTION 9

SUSQUEHANNA RIVER TO PA. RT. 944

DISTANCE: 14.6 Mi.

This section of the Trail is maintained by the Mountain Club of Maryland from the Susquehanna River to the Darlington Trail, and by the Cumberland Valley Appalachian Trail Club from the Darlington Trail to Pa. Rt. 944.

OVERVIEW OF SECTION 9

From the west end of the Clarks Ferry Bridge the first two miles are on paved roads through the town of Duncannon. A steep climb up Cove Mountain ends at Hawk Rock with outstanding views. The Trail then stays on the ridge, through the woods with rocky footing. Good views are available at the pipeline before the Trail descends to cross Pa. Rt. 850. The Trail climbs and descends Little Mountain and then climbs and descends Blue Mountain before reaching Pa. Rt. 944. Points of interest are Hawk Rock and the Darlington Shelter with a composting privy. At the crest of Blue Mountain, the Trail intersects the orange-blazed Darlington Trail and the blue-blazed Tuscarora Trail. The Darlington Trail continues 7.4 mi. northeast along Blue Mountain. The Tuscarora Trail continues 252 mi. to reconnect to the Appalachian Trail in the Shenandoah National Park in Virginia.

GENERAL INFORMATION

MAPS

Use Map #1, "A.T. in Cumberland Valley, PA (Susquehanna River to PA-94)" published by the Potomac Appalachian Trail Club.

SHELTERS AND DESIGNATED CAMPSITES

5.3 mi. from the Susquehanna River is the Cove Mountain Shelter, built in 2000 by the Mountain Club of Maryland. This shelter is the only timber frame shelter on the A.T. Look for the wood spirit carved on the end of the rafter. A seasonal spring is 400 ft. downhill on a blue-blazed trail.

12.6 mi. from the Susquehanna River is the Darlington Shelter, reconstructed in the spring of 2006 by the Mountain Club of Maryland. The spring is approximately 0.25 mi. from the shelter. A composting privy is available.

PUBLIC ACCOMMODATIONS

Duncannon offers lodging, restaurants, a laundromat, a pharmacy, and other places of business.

SUPPLIES

Supplies may be purchased in Duncannon at a number of stores.

DUNCANNON

The Borough of Duncannon takes special pride in its claim to be the approximate midpoint of the Appalachian Trail. Consequently, a special community effort is made to accommodate hikers.

CLARKS FERRY BRIDGE →

At the west end of the Clarks Ferry Bridge along U.S. Rts. 22 & 322, parking is limited. On the east end of the bridge is adequate parking along the river, adjacent to the highway that is heavily used. Parking is also available on the streets of Duncannon. An information bulletin board is at the base of the mountain next to the railroad tracks.

DUNCANNON →

There are a number of lodging opportunities, including the Doyle Hotel, and restaurants in and near Duncannon. Packages can be mailed at the post office (ZIP Code 17020).

Trail near Hawk Rock © Wayne E. Gross

N-S	**Trail Description**	S-N

0.0   **Clarks Ferry Bridge**   14.6

Southbound Hikers: From the west end of the Clarks Ferry Bridge take the first road to the left, crossing over the Juniata River and then crossing under railroad tracks. Turn right for one block on Pa. Rt. 849 (Newport Road), then turn left onto High Street.

Northbound Hikers: Reach the west end of the Clarks Ferry Bridge over the Susquehanna River. To continue on A.T. cross the bridge on pedestrian walk.

1.7   Southbound Hikers: Turn left onto Cumberland Street,   12.9
then right onto Market Street in **Duncannon**. Cross the Little Juniata Creek. Cross under U.S. Rts. 11 and 15 and then turn left on paved road passing several places of business.

Northbound Hikers: Reach the junction of Pa. Rt. 274. Trail turns right passing under U.S. Rts. 11 & 15 and continues ahead crossing the Little Juniata Creek and entering the center of **Duncannon** on Market Street. Trail then turns left onto Cumberland Street and right onto High Street. Turn right onto Pa. Rt. 849 (Newport Road). Cross under a railroad overpass and then cross the bridge over the Juniata River. See special note regarding the Borough of Duncannon at the introduction to this section.

2.1   Cross the Shermans Creek bridge.   12.5

Southbound Hikers: Continue on paved road for 0.2 mi. Trail turns sharply to the right and up an embankment. Trail ascends steeply onto the flank of Cove Mountain.

Northbound Hikers: Continue straight ahead on the paved road passing several businesses.

COVE MOUNTAIN SHELTER →

A seasonal spring is 400 ft. farther down the mountain on a blue-blazed trail.

N-S	**Trail Description**	**S-N**

2.6   Southbound Hikers: Join an old mountain road ascending the north side of the ridge.   11.9

Northbound Hikers: Old road becomes a trail which crosses the nose of Cove Mountain and descends to a paved road. Turn sharp left following the road for 0.2 mi. to Shermans Creek bridge.

3.1   Cross a rock slide.   11.5

3.4   At Hawk Rock there are fine views of the rivers, the town of Duncannon, and farmlands to compass north.   11.2

5.3   Blue-blazed trail to the east leads 500 feet to the **Cove Mountain Shelter**.   9.3

6.2   A blue-blazed trail to the west leads steeply down the mountain to the service road of the Duncannon Water Company.   8.4

7.8   Cross pipeline clearing on Cove Mountain with fine views. An unmarked trail on the west leads down the mountain to a State Game Lands parking lot.   6.8

8.9   Cross stream.   5.7

9.1   Edge of woods road.   5.5

9.4   Southbound Hikers: Trail turns right onto another woods road.   5.2

Northbound Hikers: Trail turns left onto woods road.

9.7   Southbound Hikers: A.T. turns left through woods and field.   4.9

Northbound Hikers: Turn right onto woods road.

PA. RT. 850 →

The Trail crosses Pa. Rt. 850 west of the Village of Keystone (approximately 9 mi. west of U.S. Rts. 11 & 15 at Marysville). A small A.T. parking lot with bulletin board is located on the south side of Pa. Rt. 850, 0.2 mi. east of Miller's Gap Road. There are also two State Game Lands parking areas nearby. One is located 0.4 mi. north of the highway at the end of a gravel road across from the A.T. parking lot. This parking area may be closed to the public at certain times of the year. The other is located on the south side of Pa. Rt. 850 0.4 mi. east of the A.T. parking lot.

DARLINGTON SHELTER →

A seasonal spring is approximately 0.25 mi. from the shelter. The spring is unreliable. If camping at the shelter, obtain water prior to climbing the mountain. A composting privy is provided. Composting privies must contain ONLY human waste and the supplied composting material to operate properly. The depositing of such material as cans, plastic bags, old clothing, etc., prevents the composting process. Please deposit only human waste and the toilet paper. PLEASE carry out all other trash.

DARLINGTON TRAIL →

The Darlington Trail (orange-blazed) continues 7.4 mi. northeast along Blue Mountain.

TUSCARORA TRAIL →

The Tuscarora Trail (blue-blazed) continues 252 mi. to reconnect to the Appalachian Trail in the Shenandoah National Park in Virginia.

N-S	**Trail Description**	S-N

10.3   **Pa. Rt. 850**   4.3
Southbound Hikers: Cross the road and continue across the farm field.

Northbound Hikers: Cross the road into farm field with blazed posts.

10.5   Southbound Hikers: Turn right at row of trees and follow Trail bearing diagonally to the left across the farm.   4.1

10.7   Cross Millers Gap Road.   3.9

10.8   Wooded ravine. Pass remnants of an old farmstead.   3.8

11.2   Former telephone cable clearing.   3.4

Southbound Hikers: Trail turns left and ascends Little Mountain.

11.5   Crest of Little Mountain.   3.1

11.7   Edge of woods road.   2.9

12.3   Edge of woods road.   2.3

12.6   Blue-blazed trail on east leads to the **Darlington Shelter** in approx. 200 yds.   2.0

12.7   Cross ridge top jeep road. Orange blazes mark the **Darlington Trail** to the east. The blue-blazed **Tuscarora Trail** is on the west.   1.9

13.0   Pass rock outcrop off the Trail to the west which provides a good overlook across the Cumberland Valley.   1.6

PA. RT. 944 →

The Trail crosses under Pa. Rt. 944 in a pedestrian underpass constructed in 2008. Parking here is prohibited.

Overlook across Cumberland Valley © James Foster

N-S	**Trail Description**	S-N

13.3   Edge of woods road. A seasonal spring is to the west   1.3
        just near the turn.

13.4   Edge of woods road.   1.2

13.6   Trail crosses old dirt road. Piped spring is 50 ft. to the   1.0
        west.

        Northbound Hikers: Consider getting water here.
        Darlington Shelter's seasonal spring is often dry.

14.6   **Pa. Rt. 944**, the southern end of this section, just east   0.0
        of Donnellytown.

        Southbound Hikers: Follow pedestrian underpass
        under Pa. Rt. 944.

        Northbound Hikers: The Trail proceeds toward Blue
        Mountain.

SECTION 10

PA. RT. 944 TO BOILING SPRINGS

DISTANCE: 12.3 Mi.

This section of the Trail is maintained by the Cumberland Valley Appalachian Trail Club.

OVERVIEW OF SECTION 10

From Pa. Rt. 944 the Trail goes south through woods, then reaches and follows the Conodoguinet Creek for approximately 1.5 mi. After leaving the creek, the Trail traverses a mixture of woods, farm pastures and cultivated fields on its way to Boiling Springs. Pastures and cultivated fields provide little shade, and summer hiking can be hot and dry. CARRY PLENTY OF WATER.

GENERAL INFORMATION

MAPS

Use Map #1, "A.T. in Cumberland Valley, PA (Susquehanna River to PA-94)", published by the Potomac Appalachian Trail Club.

SHELTERS AND DESIGNATED CAMPSITES

There are no shelters in this section. Camping and campfires are prohibited in this section.

PUBLIC ACCOMMODATIONS

1.2 mi.   east of the Trail on U.S. Rt. 11, in the village of New Kingstown, is a motel and deli.

0.5 mi.   west of the Trail on U.S. Rt. 11 are several motels and restaurants near the Interstate 81 interchange.

SUPPLIES

Located in Boiling Springs are a bank, post office, restaurants, convenience stores, doctors, dentist, and grocery. ATC's Mid-Atlantic Regional Office is located on the A.T. overlooking Children's Lake in Boiling Springs. Trail information is provided by staff members during office hours, 8:00 AM to 3:30 PM on weekdays. The office also has a small shop offering ATC memberships, guidebooks, maps, and associated items for sale. Hiker information and the Trail register are always available on the office's front porch.

The A.T. through Cumberland Valley © Wayne E. Gross

PA. RT. 944 ➔

The Trail crosses under Pa. Rt. 944 in a pedestrian underpass constructed in 2008. Parking here is prohibited.

SHERWOOD DRIVE ➔

One can park along the east side of Sherwood Drive.

SCOTT FARM TRAIL WORK CENTER ➔

The Scott Farm Trail Work Center is the base for the ATC's Mid-Atlantic Trail Crew. The crew builds and repairs sections of the Trail from Rockfish Gap, VA north to the NY-CT line in conjunction with the Mid-Atlantic Region A.T. Maintaining Clubs.

BERNHEISEL BRIDGE ROAD ➔

Where the A.T. leaves Bernheisel Bridge Road follow a farm lane between a baseball field and a pasture fence. Limited parking is available on the north side of the ball field along the pasture fence. Please do not block the farm lane. Limited parking is available where the Trail leaves Bernheisel Bridge south of I-81. Please do not block the farm lane which the Trail follows away from road.

For two weeks in late April or early May, depending upon the weather, a hiker can be rewarded with views of Virginia Bluebells (Mertensia virginica) wildflowers in bloom along the A.T. between Bernheisel Bridge and Sherwood Drive.

N-S	**Trail Description**	S-N

0.0   **Pa. Rt. 944,** just east of Donnellytown.   12.3
       Southbound Hikers: Follow pedestrian underpass under
       Pa. Rt. 944.

       Northbound Hikers: Continue north through woods.

0.9   **Sherwood Drive**   11.4
       Southbound Hikers: Follow road for approximately 150
       yards, before re-entering woods. For most of the next
       mile, the Trail follows alongside the Conodoguinet
       Creek.

       Northbound Hikers: Follow road for approximately 150
       yards, before re-entering woods.

2.0   Reach paved road across from the **Scott Farm Trail**   10.3
       Work Center, where potable water is available.

       Southbound Hikers: Follow the A.T. under the
       Bernheisel Bridge, then turn right and make a U-turn
       (Scott Farm Work Center is straight ahead.) onto the
       bridge.   After crossing the bridge on the attached
       pedestrian foot bridge, turn right onto boardwalk

       Northbound Hikers: Reach paved road and turn left,
       crossing the creek on pedestrian foot bridge attached to
       Bernheisel Bridge. At end of bridge make a U-turn
       then turn left under the bridge (Scott Farm Work
       Center is straight ahead.).

3.0   Cross **Bernheisel Bridge Road**.   9.3

3.4   Cross Interstate 81 on overpass.   8.9

4.3   Cross U.S. Rt. 11 on pedestrian bridge.   11.0

LISBURN ROAD ➔

Limited day use parking is available.

PA. RT. 74 ➔

Where the A.T. crosses Pa. Rt. 74 (York Road), parking is available on the north side of the road, adjacent to the west side of an old barn foundation.

BOILING SPRINGS ➔

Across from the Boiling Springs Post Office (ZIP Code 17007) is the Appalachian Trail Conservancy's Mid-Atlantic Regional Field Office along the east shore of Children's Lake. Potable water is available from an outside spigot at the rear of the ATC office, except during the coldest months of the winter.

There is limited day use parking for several cars at the Appalachian Trail Conservancy Mid-Atlantic Regional office. (Please register with office staff.) For long term or overnight parking at the nearby historical park, get permit from the ATC regional office during working hours (or call ahead during office hours at 717-258-5771 to make other arrangements). There is no overnight parking in the Pennsylvania Fish and Boat Commission parking lot on the west side of the lake.

Boiling Springs is named for the natural artesian springs in town.

N-S	**Trail Description**	S-N
5.5	Cross Pa. Turnpike (I-76) on highway overpass.	6.8
5.8	Cross Appalachian Drive.	6.5
6.5	Cross Old Stonehouse Road.	5.8
7.1	Cross Ridge Road.	5.2
8.2	Cross Trindle Road.	4.1
8.6	Cross Byers Road.	3.7
9.2	Cross **Lisburn Road**. Trail mostly follows field hedgerows in this area.	3.1
10.3	Cross **Pa. Rt. 74** (York Road).	2.0
	Southbound Hikers: The Trail traverses fields, enters woods, and reaches an area affording pastoral views.	
12.0	Pa. Rt. 174	0.3
	Southbound Hikers: Turn right, following the road into Boiling Springs.	
	Northbound Hikers: Trail turns left into woods, leaving the highway. Begin passage through alternating farm fields and wooded areas and reaches an area affording pastoral views.	
12.3	**Boiling Springs**	0.0
	Southbound Hikers: Across from the Post Office, the Trail turns left, leaving Pa. Rt. 174, and continuing south past the Appalachian Trail Conservancy Mid-Atlantic Regional Office. Potable water is available from the outside spigot at the rear of the at ATC office, except during the coldest months of winter.	

SECTION 11

BOILING SPRINGS TO PA. RT. 94

DISTANCE: 8.8 Mi.

This section of the Trail is maintained by the Cumberland Valley Appalachian Trail Club from Boiling Springs to Center Point Knob, and by the Mountain Club of Maryland from Center Point Knob to Pa. Rt. 94.

OVERVIEW OF SECTION 11

From Boiling Springs south, the Trail follows along the east shore of Children's Lake, then passes through farm fields for one mile before entering woods and beginning the climb to Center Point Knob. The last seven miles of the section are in the woods with a series of climbs and descents and elevation changes of about 500 feet. Points of interest include the lake and springs in Boiling Springs, the restored iron furnace and old mining sites, White Rocks Ridge side trail, and Rocky Ridge where the Trail passes through a maze of rock formations.

GENERAL INFORMATION

MAPS

Use Map #1, "A.T. in Cumberland Valley, PA (Susquehanna River to PA-94)", published by the Potomac Appalachian Trail Club.

SHELTERS AND DESIGNATED CAMPSITES

3.9 mi.   from Boiling Springs there is the Alec Kennedy Shelter.

0.3 mi.   from Boiling Springs is a designated backpacker campsite with port-a-potty in season. Campfires are prohibited. Potable water is available from the outside spigot at the rear of the ATC office, except during the coldest months of winter.

PUBLIC ACCOMMODATIONS

Bed and breakfast inns and restaurants are located in the village of Boiling Springs.

There are motels and restaurants in the town of Mount Holly Springs, located 2.5 mi. north of the A.T. on Pa. Rt. 34 and in Carlisle, 5 mi. northwest of Boiling Springs or 5 mi. north of Mount Holly Springs.

SUPPLIES

Located in Boiling Springs are a bank, post office, restaurants, convenience stores, doctors, dentist, and grocery. ATC's Mid-Atlantic Regional Office is located on the A.T. overlooking Children's Lake in Boiling Springs. Trail information is provided by staff members during office hours, 8:00 AM to 3:30 PM on weekdays. The office also has a small shop offering ATC memberships, guidebooks, maps, and associated items for sale. Hiker information and the Trail register are always available on the office's front porch.

Supplies can also be purchased in the town of Mount Holly Springs.

Most major services are available in Carlisle.

BOILING SPRINGS →

Across from the Boiling Springs Post Office (ZIP Code 17007) is the Appalachian Trail Conservancy's Mid-Atlantic Regional Field Office along the east shore of Children's Lake. Potable water is available from an outside spigot at the rear of the ATC office, except during the coldest months of the winter.

There is limited day use parking for several cars at the Appalachian Trail Conservancy Mid-Atlantic Regional office. (Please register with office staff.) For long term or overnight parking at the nearby historical park, get permit from the ATC regional office during working hours (or call ahead during office hours at 717-258-5771 to make other arrangements). There is no overnight parking in the Pennsylvania Fish and Boat Commission parking lot by the lake.

Boiling Springs is named for the natural artesian springs in town.

BACKPACKER CAMPSITE →

Campfires are prohibited.

LEIDIGH ROAD →

Limited day use parking available.

CENTER POINT KNOB →

Center Point Knob was once the mid point of the A.T.

WHITE ROCKS RIDGE TRAIL →

The White Rocks Ridge Trail (former A.T.) follows the ridge, winding through and over outcroppings of hard quartzite rock, dating back some 550 million years. White Rocks forms one of the outlines of the greater South Mountain and marks the northern terminus of the Blue Ridge Mountains. The Trail is rough and rocky, and slippery in wet weather. The White Rocks Ridge Trail leads 1.3 mi. to Kuhn Road.

ALEC KENNEDY SHELTER →

Shelter is 850 feet from the A.T.

N-S	**Trail Description**	**S-N**

0.0   Pa. Rt. 174   **Boiling Springs**   8.8

Southbound Hikers: The Trail leads south past the Regional Office, and then follows along the east shore of Children's Lake. Beyond the lake, cross the road into a township park with a restored iron furnace.

Northbound Hikers: To continue north, turn right and follow Pa. Rt. 174.

0.3   Cross Yellow Breeches Creek (a notable trout stream)   8.5
on a stone arch highway bridge. The only designated **Backpacker Campsite** in the Cumberland Valley A.T. section is past the gate, down an old road to the east next to the railroad tracks.

Southbound Hikers: Cross very active railroad tracks, bear left off paved road past a gate into farm fields follow blazed posts.

Northbound Hikers: Go through a township park with a restored iron furnace, and then follow along the east shore of Children's Lake.

1.1   Cross **Leidigh Road**.   7.7

Cultivated field with blazed post is to the south side of the road.

1.7   Pass evidence of old mine operations.   7.1

3.0   Reach **Center Point Knob**, the one-time mid-point of   5.8
the A.T. On southern side of summit, within 100 yards, reach blue-blazed **White Rocks Ridge Trail** leading east 1.3 mi. to Kuhn Road.

3.9   A blue-blazed trail leads east to the **Alec Kennedy**   4.9
Shelter, 850 feet from the A.T.

WHISKEY SPRINGS ROAD ➜

There is limited parking along the side of Whiskey Springs Road.

SHEET IRON ROOF ROAD ➜

There is parking along the side of Sheet Iron Roof Road.

PA. RT. 94 ➜

There is very limited parking at Pa. Rt. 94. Do not trespass. There is a parking for several cars a short distance away on Sheet Iron Roof Road, and at a parking lot on Pa. Rt. 34 0.1 mi. south of the trail crossing.

Yellow Breeches Creek Bridge © Thomas Scully

N-S	**Trail Description**	S-N
4.0	Cross a woods road with orange blazes, which to the east leads 1.7 mi. to Boy Scout Camp Tuckahoe. Cross Little Dogwood Run. Pass through an old charcoal hearth.	4.8
4.8	Cross a pipeline that looks like a narrow road.	4.0
5.5	Pass a rock outcrop on the east with a view.	3.3
6.0	**Whiskey Springs Road** and pass Whiskey Spring in 30 yds, which is always flowing.	2.8
6.2	Crest of Rocky Ridge through a maze of rock formations.	2.6
7.0	Pass vista on the west.	1.8
	Southbound Hikers: A.T. descends Rocky Ridge by switchbacks.	
7.4	Cross Old Town Road (dirt road).	1.4
7.5	Cross old road.	1.3
7.8	Southbound Hikers: Cross old road, telephone line right-of-way, and stream.	1.2
	Northbound Hikers: Cross above items in reverse.	
7.9	Trail turns at junction.	1.1
8.1	Cross stream.	0.7
8.6	Cross **Sheet Iron Roof Road**.	0.2
8.7	Cross under a power line.	0.1
8.8	**Pa. Rt. 94**	0.0

SECTION 12

PA. RT. 94 TO PINE GROVE FURNACE

DISTANCE: 10.9 Mi.

This section of the Trail is maintained by the Mountain Club of Maryland.

OVERVIEW OF SECTION 12

This section is generally in the woods for the entire route. After leaving Pa. Rt. 94, climb and descend Trents Hill, then ascend Piney Mountain, walking along the ridge before descending to Pine Grove Furnace State Park. Points of interest are the sheer, conspicuous quartzite cliffs and splendid view of the lakes at Pole Steeple, 0.5 mi. off the Trail atop Piney Mountain; and the ruins of the old Pine Grove Furnace. The park office houses a small, but interesting, museum of the natural and industrial history of the area.

GENERAL INFORMATION

MAPS

Use Map #2-3, "AT in Michaux State Forest, Pa (PA-94 to US-30)" published by the Potomac Appalachian Trail Club.

HUNTERS RUN ROAD

The road referred to in this section as "Hunters Run Road" is shown on some maps as Pine Grove Road, and an occasional sign to that effect may still be encountered.

SHELTERS AND DESIGNATED CAMPSITES

3.3 mi.   from Pa. Rt. 94 is a blue-blazed trail leading 0.2 mi. to the Tagg Run Shelter with a raised sleeping platform. A spring is 100 feet beyond the shelters. A composting outhouse facility is at the site.

PUBLIC ACCOMMODATIONS

There are motels and restaurants in Mount Holly Springs, 2.5 mi. north of the Trail from both Pa. Rt. 94 and Pa. Rt. 34. Pine Grove Furnace State Park offers campsites and swimming facilities. There is also a seasonal snack bar in the Park. The Ironmaster's Mansion Hostel of American Youth Hostels is also in the park on Pa. Rt. 233 and the A.T.

SUPPLIES

Supplies may be purchased in Mount Holly Springs. A general store is 0.25 mi. from the Trail near intersection of Pa. Rt. 34 and Hunters Run Road. In Pine Grove Furnace State Park there is a seasonal small store 50 yards off the Trail near the Ironmaster's Mansion Hostel on the south side of Pa. Rt. 233. The store is generally open seven days a week between Memorial Day and Labor Day. There are two public campgrounds located west of the trail along Pine Grove Road; Cherokee Campground (0.4 mi.) has a small camp store and snack bar which is open year round. Mountain Creek Campground (1.4 mi.) has a camp store.

PA. RT. 94 →

There is very limited parking at Pa. Rt. 94. Do not trespass. There is a parking for several cars a short distance away on Sheet Iron Roof Road, and at a parking lot on Pa. Rt. 34 0.1 mi. south of the trail crossing.

The mountain laurel along the footpath in this area is covered with blossoms in June.

There are many sassafras trees and blueberry bushes in this section.

PA. RT. 34 →

Trail crosses PA. Rt. 34. Parking is available 0.1 mi. south of Trail crossing.

HUNTERS RUN ROAD →

The Trail crosses Hunters Run Road. Very limited parking.

TAGG RUN SHELTER →

Tagg Run Shelter has a spring 100 feet beyond on blue-blazed trail. Do not drink water from Tagg Run; cows pasturing upstream cause contamination.

N-S	**Trail Description**	S-N
0.0	**Pa. Rt. 94**	10.9

Southbound Hikers: Enter the woods and ascend to a woods road on Trents Hill.

Northbound Hikers: A.T. continues across highway and into the woods.

0.2	Turn at northern end of woods road.	10.7
0.4	Turn at southern end of woods road.	10.5
1.1	Turn in Trail. Trents Hill.	9.8
1.8	**Pa. Rt. 34**	9.1

Southbound Hikers: Turn left, cross stream on highway bridge, and bear right into a field. Turn left on Trail through woods to field. Cross field into woods. Cross the railroad track and bear left along old rail bed.

Northbound Hikers: A.T. turns left, crosses stream on highway bridge, and turns right.

2.9	Cross **Hunters Run Road**.	8.0
3.2	Cross Tagg Run. A blue-blazed trail to the east leads 0.2 mi. to the **Tagg Run Shelter**.	7.7
3.5	Turn in Trail.	7.4
4.6	Blue-blazed trail (not maintained) to the west leads downhill 0.7 mi. to Hunters Run Road and Mountain Creek Campground.	6.3
4.9	Cross Limekiln Road, a woods road. To the east, it leads to the Village of Goodyear. To the west, it leads 0.9 mi. downhill to Hunters Run Road.	6.0

POLE STEEPLE →

Blue-blazed trail to the west leads 0.5 mi. to Pole Steeple, a cliff with a great view. From there a blue-blazed trail descends the cliff face and in 0.6 mi. reaches a multiuse trail that leads to Fuller Lake.

PINE GROVE FURNACE STATE PARK →

In Pine Grove Furnace State Park, there is adequate parking. Contact the Park Office for regulations governing the extended parking of vehicles. Pass Ironmaster's Mansion American Youth Hostel on the west. A seasonal grocery store is in the white building on the west. The Trail passes through the picnic grounds. Note the ruins of the old Pine Grove Furnace.

Pine Grove Furnace was acquired by the Watts family, who established a furnace, a forge, coal house, brick mansion house, smith and carpenter shops, 30 log dwellings, and grist and saw mills. The operation was supported by the charcoal that was produced from some 35,000 acres of land. Throughout this area are more of the charcoal hearths.

Most of the structures associated with the Pine Grove Furnace were destroyed by fire in 1915. All that survived were the mansion house, and the furnace. The railroad that serviced these works in the 1870s followed Mountain Creek up from Laurel Lake. This is the roadbed that is now used by the A.T. as it passes Fuller Lake, which was originally a 90-foot deep ore hole. Following a pump breakdown, the mine was flooded and later abandoned. Soon after 1893, the entire iron works operation closed down.

The Grist Mill will be the home of the Appalachian Trail Museum. The opening is scheduled for June 5, 2010, National Trails Day. Contact at www.atmuseum.org. The Appalachian Trail Museum Society serves the Appalachian Trail community by telling the stories of the founding, construction, preservation, maintenance, protection, and enjoyment of the Trail since its creation.

N-S	**Trail Description**	S-N
5.9	Turn at a junction with a blue-blazed trail (not maintained) which comes up from Hunters Run Road.	5.0
8.0	Old Forge Road (woods road) on Piney Mountain. Blue-blazed trail to **Pole Steeple.**	2.9
9.5	Southbound Hikers: Turn left onto the old railroad bed, now a park multiuse path leading to Fuller Lake.	1.4
	Northbound Hikers: Turn right ascending an old mountain road known as Petersburg Road.	
10.1	Cross foot bridge, turn, and cross another foot bridge.	0.8
10.5	Locked gate. Southbound Hikers: Continuing through the park, note the ruins of the old Pine Grove Furnace on your right.	0.4
	Northbound Hikers: Continue past the locked gate on an old railroad bed, now a park multi use path, passing Fuller Lake on the right.	
10.6	Bendersville Road and **Pine Grove Furnace State Park**.	0.3
10.9	Bendersville Lane. Pass Ironmaster's Mansion American Youth Hostel on the west. Southbound Hikers Bear left on Pa Rt 233 along the highway for 200 yards and then turn right onto road.	0.0

SECTION 13

PINE GROVE FURNACE TO CALEDONIA

DISTANCE: 19.7 Mi.

This section of the Trail is maintained by the North Chapter of the Potomac Appalachian Trail Club.

OVERVIEW OF SECTION 13

Leaving Pine Grove Furnace State Park the first six miles is a gradual ascent to the plateau-like top of South Mountain, then along the plateau with minor changes in elevation to a rather steep descent to Caledonia State Park. This section achieves the highest elevations on the A.T. in Pennsylvania at about 2,000 feet. Points of interest along the Trail are the preserved ruins of the old iron furnace in Pine Grove Furnace State Park and the small but interesting museum depicting the natural and industrial history of the area. One passes many circular flat charcoal burning hearths, 30 to 50 feet in diameter. See the Chapter on History.

In the former Camp Michaux property, the Trail passes the one remaining wall of a huge stone barn dating from the early days. For several years Keystone Trails Association held its fall meeting at this church camp. In World War II it had been a prisoner-of-war camp for captured German submarine personnel, and before that, a CCC Camp. The Trail shelters and the Milesburn Cabin were built by the CCC about 1935.

A model iron furnace and the Thaddeus Stevens Museum are along U.S. Rt. 30 in Caledonia State Park, 0.6 mi. east of the Trail.

This section is located mainly in Michaux State Forest. Therefore, all rules and regulations must be followed.

GENERAL INFORMATION

MAPS

Use Map #2-3, "AT in Michaux State Forest, Pa (PA-94 to US-30)" published by the Potomac Appalachian Trail Club.

Special .Note: *The Trail crosses many unimproved roads in this section, most of which are maintenance roads of the Michaux State Forest. Limited parking is possible at many of these crossings, but vandalism is an occasional problem. Check ATC's website for parking tips at every Trailhead, including any reports of vandalism.*

SHELTERS AND DESIGNATED CAMPSITES

3.4 mi.   from Pine Grove Furnace State Park are the twin Toms Run Shelters.

6.5 mi.   from Pine Grove Furnace State Park is the Anna Michener Memorial Cabin of the PATC. This is a locked cabin with the capacity of 14 persons. Reservations to rent must be obtained in advance from the Potomac Appalachian Trail Club, 118 Park Street, SE, Vienna, VA 22180; telephone 703-242-0693 weekday evenings; www.patc.org.

9.7 mi.   from Pine Grove Furnace State Park is Birch Run Shelter.

12.1 mi.   from Pine Grove Furnace State Park is the Milesburn Cabin of the PATC. This is a locked cabin with a capacity of 12 persons. Reservations to rent must be obtained in advance from PATC.

17.0 mi. from Pine Grove Furnace State Park is Quarry Gap Shelter.

PUBLIC ACCOMMODATIONS

There is a seasonal snack bar at Fuller Lake in Pine Grove Furnace State Park. The Ironmaster's Mansion Hostel (AYH) is open year round in un the park. There are two public campgrounds located west of the trail along Pine Grove Road; Cherokee Campground (0.4 mi.) has a small camp store and snack bar which is open year round. Mountain Creek Campground (1.4 mi.) has a camp store

There is a seasonal snack bar at the swimming pool in Caledonia State Park. East of Caledonia State Park, along U.S. Rt. 30, is a restaurant within a mile; and in 2.1 mi., Colonel's Creek Campground where cabins can be rented. To the west on U.S. Rt. 30, 2.5 mi., is the Rite Spot Motel and Restaurant.

SUPPLIES

In Pine Grove Furnace State Park there is a seasonal small store 50 yards off the Trail near the Ironmaster's Mansion Hostel on the south side of Pa. Rt. 233. The store is generally open seven days a week between Memorial Day and Labor Day.

There is a grocery store 0.9 mi. west of Caledonia State Park along U.S. Rt. 30. There is a pizza shop 0.5 mi. west of the park. In the village of South Mountain, about 5.0 mi. south of Caledonia State Park and 1.1 mi. east of the Trail, along Sanatorium Road, is located a grocery store and gas station, as well as a post office.

N-S	**Trail Description**	S-N

0.0   Pa. Rt. 233   **19.7**

Southbound Hikers: The Trail leaves Pa. Rt. 233 about 200 yds south of the Ironmaster's Mansion Hostel turn right onto a paved road.

Northbound Hikers: Reach Pa. Rt. 233 and turn left for about 200 yards, then turn right onto Bendersville Lane entering Pine Grove Furnace State Park. The first road to the left passes the seasonally operated park store, an old white building in 50 yds, and continues on to the park headquarters building which is located on Pa. Rt. 233.

0.1   Southbound Hikers: Where the gravel road ends, bear right and in 40 yds bear left onto an old woods road.   **19.6**

Turn right onto a gravel road.

0.7   Pass several charcoal flats which provided fuel for Pine Grove Furnace in the 1700's.   **19.0**

Southbound Hikers: Leave the woods road.

1.5   Northbound Hikers: Cross a small brook, then pass old charcoal flats which provided fuel for Pine Grove Furnace in the 1700's. Trail bears right, then left.   **18.6**

1.3   Blue-blazed Sunset Rocks Trail leads to the east. (For detailed Trail data see the end of this section.) Parking lot is at end of Old Shippensburg Road 50 yds on west.   **18.4**

Southbound Hikers: Continuing straight ahead in 30 yards cross Toms Run on foot bridge and turn left onto Old Shippensburg Road.

Northbound Hikers: A.T. bears right crossing Toms Run on a footbridge.

Ironmaster's Mansion Hostel © Lorrie Preston

MICHAUX ROAD

The Trail crosses Michaux Road, also called High Mountain Road, at the site of the former Camp Michaux. Limited parking. No protection from vandalism.

To the east, off Michaux Road, is a carved rock plaque noting that Camp Michaux was the site of a World War II prisoner of war camp.

TOMS RUN SHELTERS

Privy and Spring are behind shelters.

N-S	**Trail Description**	S-N

1.6   Short trail to the east leads 50 yards to Halfway Spring.   18.1

2.0   The clearing is the site of the former Camp Michaux and the ruins of a large stone barn.   17.6

     Southbound Hikers: A.T. turns right onto **Michaux Road**, also called High Mountain Road.

2.1   Southbound Hikers: Trail turns left onto a woods road.   17.4

     Northbound Hikers: Turn right onto Michaux Road, also called High Mountain Road, then passing into the site of the former Camp Michaux.

3.4   Reach the twin **Toms Run Shelters**.   16.3

3.5   Blue-blazed Sunset Rocks Trail on the east. (For detailed Trail data see the end of this section.)   16.2

     Northbound Hikers: After crossing Toms Run the blue-blazed Sunset Rocks Trail comes in from the left. A.T. now ascends the steep slope of Antmire Hill.

4.6   Cross Woodrow Road, a forestry road passable by auto. Fine views.   15.1

5.2   Boundary of the private Tumbling Run Game Preserve.   14.5

     Southbound Hikers: Turn right, paralleling Ridge Road which is a short distance to the right. (CAUTION: Do not follow the Michaux Forest boundary markers, which are also white paint.) No camping or fires in the preserve.

Rhododendron tunnel on the Trail © Wayne E. Gross

ARENDTSVILLE-SHIPPENSBURG ROAD ➔

The Trail crosses the Arendtsville-Shippensburg Road. Parking. No protection from vandalism.

BIRCH RUN SHELTER ➔

Spring is to the west of the shelter.

N-S	**Trail Description**	**S-N**

5.9   Cross the entrance road to the Preserve.   13.8

Southbound Hikers: Leave Preserve land.

Northbound Hikers: Cross the entrance road to the private Tumbling Run Game Preserve. No camping or fires in the preserve. Trail turns right, then left, generally following the boundary of the game preserve.

6.5   Blue-blazed trail to the east leads 0.2 mi. to the locked   13.2
       Anna Michener Memorial Cabin of the PATC.

7.3   Cross the old bed of Dead Woman Hollow Road, now   12.4
       a winter snowmobile trail.

Northbound Hikers: A long descent is ahead with views of Mount Holly and Long Mountain in the distance.

8.3   Cross the **Arendtsville-Shippensburg Road**. Limited   11.4
       parking is available.

9.7   **Birch Run Shelter**. Cross Birch Run north of shelter.   10.0

10.3 Cross the old bed of Fegley Hollow Road. Powerline,   9.4
       crossing is south of the road crossing.

11.0 Cross Michaux Forest's Rocky Knob Trail, a loop   8.7
       nature trail to the east. Ridge Road is a short distance
       to the west.

11.7 Cross Ridge Road.   8.0

Quarry Gap Shelter © James Stauch

HOSACK RUN TRAIL ➔

Hosack Run Trail is on the east and joins the Locust Gap Trail in 1.1 mi. (In combination with the A.T., this provides a beautiful circuit hike).

QUARRY GAP SHELTER ➔

Spring is located 10 yds in front of shelter. Nearby is Locked Antlers camp hunting club, which was founded in 1890.

N-S	**Trail Description**	S-N
12.1	Milesburn Road. The locked Milesburn Cabin of the PATC is on the south side of road crossing. A blue-blazed trail to the west leads downstream and across Milesburn Road to a spring.	7.6
12.5	Cross the intersection of Canada Hollow Road, Means Hollow Road, and Ridge Road.	7.2
12.9	Cross Dughill Trail.	6.8
13.0	Cross Middle Ridge Road.	6.7
14.4	Cross old woods road.	5.3
14.8	Cross a power line cut.	4.9
15.6	Reach the junction of Ridge Road and Stillhouse Road in an area known as Sandy Sod.	4.1
	Southbound Hikers: A.T. goes ahead on Ridge Road for 0.1 mi. then turns left into the woods and descends through Quarry Gap.	
	Northbound Hikers: Reach the top of the hill and turn right onto Ridge Road.	
16.3	**Hosack Run Trail** is on the east.	3.4
16.8	A.T. crosses a stream.	2.9
17.0	Arrive at the **Quarry Gap Shelter.**	2.7
17.4	Pass the former Locked Antlers Camp on the east. The A.T. is gated here to control vehicle access to the Quarry Gap Shelter.	2.3

CALEDONIA STATE PARK ➔

In Caledonia State Park there is adequate parking. Contact the Park Office for location and for regulations governing the extended parking of vehicles.

Thaddeus Stevens owned the land that is now Caledonia State Park. He built the iron furnace in 1837. Thaddeus Stevens is known as the father of the public school system in Pennsylvania. He served as a member of the U.S. House of Representatives and was a noted abolitionist. Confederate Cavalry destroyed his iron furnace under the leadership of Jubal Early in July 1863. The fields around the furnace were used as field hospitals during the Battle of Gettysburg. The land was sold to the state and became a state park in 1903.

U.S. RT. 30 ➔

The Trail crosses U.S. Rt. 30 0.6 mi. west of the intersection of U.S. Rt. 30 with Pa. Rt. 233. Adequate parking is nearby. Contact Caledonia State Park office for regulations governing the extended parking of vehicles. Michaux District Forester's office is 0.4 mi. beyond. To the west 0.9 mi. are two stores, a motel, and restaurant in an additional 1.6 mi.

N-S	**Trail Description**	S-N

17.7   Southbound Hikers: Turn right off Quarry Gap Road onto Greenwood Furnace Road.   2.0

17.9   Pass the blue-blazed Caledonia Park Three Valley Trail.   1.8

Southbound Hikers: Where the Locust Gap Trail continues ahead, the A.T. turns left.

Northbound Hikers: Climb steeply between Orebank Hill on the left and Chinquapin Hill on the right.

18.8   Cross a wide park maintenance road. Pass two parking lots and a seasonal restroom in **Caledonia State Park**. (Reverse for Northbound hikers.) The road leads east to the park office in 0.4 mi.   0.7

19.1   Cross Conococheague Creek on Caledonia Park bridge.   0.4

Southbound Hikers: A.T. bears to the right.

19.4   Cross bridge over former canal.   0.1

19.5   Reach **U.S. Rt. 30**.   0.0

DETAILED TRAIL DATA

SUNSET ROCKS TRAIL
(Blue-blazed trail)

N-S	Trail Description	S-N
0.0	Where the A.T. crosses Toms Run, the blue-blazed Sunset Rocks Trail keeps to the east of the run following a former woods road.	2.4
0.4	Crest of Little Rocky Ridge and Sunset Rocks.	2.0
	Southbound Hikers: Turn left from the ridge crest and descend. A short spur trail goes straight ahead to an excellent view.	
	Northbound Hikers: Turn right (to the left, a short spur trail provides excellent views) and follow through and up over boulders. Use care!	
1.1	Michaux (High Mountain) Road.	1.3
1.4	Edge of paved road and wire fence of the former Camp Michaux.	1.0
2.4	A.T. at 3.5 mi. from Pa. Rt. 233 in Pine Grove Furnace Park.	0.0
	Southbound Hikers: Shelters are another 30 yds to the west.	
	Northbound Hikers: From A.T. follow blue-blazed trail.	

Thaddeus Stevens Blacksmith Shop © Lorrie Preston

SECTION 14

CALEDONIA TO PEN MAR

DISTANCE: 17.9 Mi.

This section of the Trail is maintained by the North Chapter of the Potomac Appalachian Trail Club.

OVERVIEW OF SECTION 14

Most of the Trail in this section is through pleasing woods on Rocky Mountain. The main climb to Snowy Mountain is gradual with a descent to the Old Forge Picnic Grounds area, and a steep climb up to Pen Mar. Watch for the white paint boundary markings of Michaux State Forest Lands, which cross the A.T. and are similar to A.T. blazes, causing some confusion. A.T. white blazes are 2" X 6" and face the hiker. State Forest markings, also white, are quite irregular. Points of interest along the Trail are the Chimney Rocks and the Old Forge Picnic Ground.

This section is mainly located in Michaux State Forest. All rules and regulations must be followed.

GENERAL INFORMATION

MAPS

Use Map #4, "AT in Michaux State Forest, Pa (US-30 to PA-MD State Line)" published by the Potomac Appalachian Trail Club.

SHELTERS AND DESIGNATED CAMPSITES

3.0 mi. from Caledonia State Park are the Rocky Mountain Shelters on a side trail to the east. These have replaced the former Raccoon Run Shelters

8.3 mi. from Caledonia State Park is the locked Hermitage Cabin of the PATC, located 0.9 mi. off the Trail. Reservations to rent must be obtained in advance from the Potomac Appalachian Trail Club, 118 Park Street, SE, Vienna, VA 22180; telephone 703-242-0693 weekday evenings; www.patc.org.

9.6 mi. from Caledonia State Park there are the two Tumbling Run Shelters along the Trail.

10.8 mi. from Caledonia State Park is the Antietam Shelter just beyond the Old Forge Picnic Grounds.

13.2 mi. from Caledonia State Park are the two Deer Lick Shelters.

PUBLIC ACCOMMODATIONS

There is a seasonal snack bar at the swimming pool in Caledonia State Park. East of Caledonia State Park, along U.S. Rt. 30, is a restaurant within a mile; and in 2.1 mi., Colonel's Creek Campground where cabins can be rented. To the west on U.S. Rt. 30, 2.5 mi., is the Rite Spot Motel and Restaurant. There is one restaurant in Blue Ridge Summit, 1.8 mi. east of the Trail on Pa. Rt. 16.

SUPPLIES

There is a grocery store 0.9 mi. west of Caledonia State Park along U.S. Rt. 30. There is a pizza shop 0.5 mi. west of the park. In the village of South Mountain, about 5.0 mi. south of Caledonia State Park and 1.1 mi. east of the Trail, along Sanatorium Road, is located a grocery store and gas station, as well as a post office. Along Pa. Rt. 16, there are stores in Rouzerville 2.5 mi. west of the Trail and in Blue Ridge Summit 1.8 mi. east of the Trail.

U.S. RT. 30 →

The Trail crosses U.S. Rt. 30 0.6 mi. west of the intersection of U.S. Rt. 30 with Pa. Rt. 233. Adequate parking is nearby. Contact Caledonia State Park office for regulations governing the extended parking of vehicles. Michaux District Forester's office is 0.4 mi. beyond. To the west 0.9 mi. are two stores, a motel, and restaurant in an additional 1.6 mi.

ROCKY MOUNTAIN SHELTERS →

The blue-blazed trail continues another 0.26 mi. To Pa. Rt. 223. The spring is another 0.1 mi. south on the west side of Pa. Rt. 233.

PA. RT. 233 →

Trail crosses Pa. Rt. 233. Limited parking. No protection from vandals. To the east 1.6 mi. is the village of South Mountain, with store and post office. Pa. Rt. 233 goes north to Caledonia State Park and U.S. Rt. 30. To the west Pa. Rt. 233 goes to the village of Mont Alto, Mont Alto School of Forestry of Penn State University, and Mont Alto State Park. Vision Quest Camp entrance is visible 100 yards to the east.

CHIMNEY ROCKS →

The blue-blazed trail to the east leads 120 yds to Chimney Rocks, at 1,940 feet of elevation, with a magnificent view over Green Ridge and the Waynesboro Reservoir. Blue-blazed trail to the west leads 1.2 mi. down to the locked Hermitage Cabin of the PATC. (Reservations to rent must be obtained in advance from PATC. See Shelters in General Information.)

TUMBLING RUN SHELTERS →

Tumbling Run Shelters are 30 yds to the west. In 105 yds a blue-blazed trail leads back through the shelter area and in 0.6 mi. to the PATC Hermitage Cabin.

N-S	**Trail Description**	S-N
0.0	Cross **U.S. Rt. 30**.	17.9
0.1	Cross gas pipe line clearing.	17.8
3.0	Blue-blazed side trail to the east goes downhill 0.3 mi. to the **Rocky Mountain Shelters**.	14.9
4.5	Cross a gravel maintenance road on ridge leading east 0.1 mi. to water tanks.	13.4
4.7	Reach **Pa. Rt. 233**.	13.2
4.9	Unmarked trail to east goes to Caledonia State Park.	13.0
5.0	Southbound Hiker: Turn onto Swamp Road through a very boggy area.	12.9
5.1	Northbound Hiker: Turn onto Swamp Road through a very boggy area.	12.8
5.4	Cross dirt road (closed to public).	12.5
5.7	Cross Snowy Mountain Road.	12.2
6.3	Cross under a power line.	11.6
7.5	Cross a pipeline.	10.4
8.3	Near summit of Buzzard Peak reach intersection with blue-blazed trail that leads east to **Chimney Rocks** and west to PATC Hermitage Cabin.	9.6
9.6	**Tumbling Run Shelters** are 30 yds to the west.	8.3

OLD FORGE ROAD →

The Trail crosses Old Forge Road near the Old Forge Picnic Ground. Limited parking.

OLD FORGE PICNIC GROUNDS →

The Trail reaches the edge of the playing field of Old Forge Picnic Grounds. Parking is available for approximately 10 vehicles. Overnight parking must be permitted by Michaux State Forest office.

ANTIETAM SHELTER →

Antietam Shelter is to the east. Do not drink water from the Antietam Creek. Water is obtainable in the summer months from the fountains at the picnic grounds. If approach to the bridge area is flooded return to Rattlesnake Run Road and follow blue-blazed trail around to the other side of the footbridges.

DEER LICK SHELTERS →

Arrive at Deer Lick Shelters and spring on the east. A second spring is 0.25 mi. on blue-blazed trail from the front of the shelters.

N-S	**Trail Description**	**S-N**

9.8   Reach paved **Old Forge Road**.   8.1

Southbound Hikers: Turn right across bridge, then left into woods.

10.4   Cross Rattlesnake Run Road. A blue-blazed trail   7.5
follows road to east for 0.2 mi. This blue-blazed trail is a high-water route in case the approaches to Antietam Shelter are not passable.

Southbound Hikers: Enter woods to right, and in another 0.2 mi. rejoins A.T. beyond footbridges at 10.8/7.1 mi.

10.7   Reach edge of **Old Forge Picnic Grounds**. Frost free   7.2
water tap is on side of well house immediately to right.

Southbound Hikers: A.T. turns left and in 0.1 mi. turns right for 50 yds through a pipeline clearing before reentering woods.

Northbound Hikers: Trail turns right and reenters woods.

10.8   Two footbridges for crossing East Branch of Antietam   7.1
Creek with **Antietam Shelter** to the east.

12.3   Cross woods road. Rattlesnake Run Road is 0.17 mi.   5.6
to the east.

12.9   Cross a pipeline clearing. Rattlesnake Run Road is   5.0
0.15 mi. to the east.

13.2   Pass **Deer Lick Shelters** and spring on the east.   4.7

PA RT. 16 →

The Trail crosses PA Rt. 16 between Rouzerville and Blue Ridge Summit. Limited parking.

MICHAUX STATE FOREST →

The Michaux State Forest is named in honor of André Michaux. He was a famous French botanist dispatched by the King and Queen of France in 1785 to gather plants for the Royal Gardens. He befriended William Bartram, the leading American botanist, who lived in Philadelphia. André Michaux went on many solo expeditions to explore the wilderness of eastern United States. He and his son Francois André Michaux are noted for discovering and identifying many flowers, shrubs and trees.

The 85,000-acre Michaux State Forest is located in Adams, Cumberland and Franklin counties.

In 1902 the first forest tree nursery in Pennsylvania was established in Mont Alto in the Michaux State Forest. The first wooden fire tower was established in 1905 and the first steel fire tower in 1914. In 1903 the first Forest Academy in Pennsylvania was established at Mont Alto. It was only the second one in the nation to train professional foresters. Prior to that, foresters went to Europe for training.

N-S	**Trail Description**	S-N

14.5   Reach Bailey Spring 15 yds off the Trail on the west.   3.4
It is an excellent walled spring and always flowing.

Southbound Hikers: A.T. goes left from spring for 25
yds then right uphill.   Use care following blazes due
to State Forest boundary blazes and old woods roads.

14.7   Cross Rattlesnake Run Road.   3.2

15.1   Follow Mentzer Gap Road for 70 yds.   2.8

15.3   Trail reaches Pa. Rt. 16. Rouzerville is 2.1 mi. west;   2.6
Blue Ridge Summit is 1.8 mi. east.

Southbound Hikers: A.T. crosses Pa. Rt. 16, then
crosses Red Run by a log bridge and leaves the
southern boundary of **Michaux State Forest**.

15.6   Cross old **Pa. Rt. 16**.   2.3

Southbound Hikers: Ascend, and then descend Mount
Dunlop.

Northbound Hikers: A.T. soon crosses southern
boundary of **Michaux State Forest** and crosses Red
Run on log bridge.

16.8   Cross Buena Vista Road with roadside spring on the   1.1
west.   Several miles to the west is the site of the
former Buena Vista Hotel.

17.3   Cross Falls Creek on trail bridge.   0.7

PEN MAR PARK →

During summer season restrooms in the park are open. The park was constructed by Colonel J.M. Hood of the Western Maryland Railroad in 1871 and remained for more than 60 years one of the most famous resorts in the East. The Western Maryland Railway ran many excursion trains here, bringing clubs, Sunday School picnic groups, and similar organizations for a summer outing. A feature of the park was an observatory platform at High Rock, from which Chambersburg could be seen 24 mi. in the distance. The park also included a fun house, a roller coaster, a miniature railroad, resort hotels, and restaurants. It is said that the average attendance for such picnics was 7,000 people, with the record having been set by a Lutheran gathering that numbered 15,000.

MASON-DIXON LINE →

The Mason-Dixon marker for Mile 91, from the 1765 survey, is on private property and is no longer accessible from the A.T. Between 1763 and 1767 Charles Mason and Jeremiah Dixon surveyed the border between Pennsylvania and Maryland to resolve a dispute between the Province of Pennsylvania and the Province of Maryland. Both Provinces claimed land between the 39th and 40th parallels according to the charters granted to each colony. The survey line is marked by stones every mile and by crownstones every five miles. The Pennsylvania side of each crownstone has the coat of arms of the Penn family and Maryland side has the coat of arms of the Calvert family.

The Mason-Dixon Line became known as the border between northern and southern states.

PEN MAR →

The Trail goes through the village of Pen Mar. Limited parking. Do not trespass. Parking is available in Pen Mar County Park in Maryland.

N-S	**<u>Trail Description</u>**	S-N

17.4   Pass old stone wall on west. Cross old trolley line   0.5
        road bed which once served **Pen Mar Park**.

17.7   Southbound Hikers: Turn right onto power line right-   0.2
        of-way.

        Northbound Hikers: Turn left off power line right-of-
        way and descend into woods.

17.8   Cross Pen Mar Road.   0.1

17.9   **Mason-Dixon Line. Pen Mar.**   0.0

        Southbound Hikers: Enter Maryland and in 50 yds
        cross railroad tracks. A.T. then bears right in 0.2 mi.
        Reach center of Washington County's Pen Mar Park.
        See *The   Appalachian   Trail   Guide   to
        Maryland/Northern Virginia.*

        Northbound Hikers: Enter Pennsylvania. (From center
        of Pen Mar Park A.T. reaches state line by descending
        0.2 mi., crossing railroad tracks, and preceding
        another 50 yds.)

INDEX

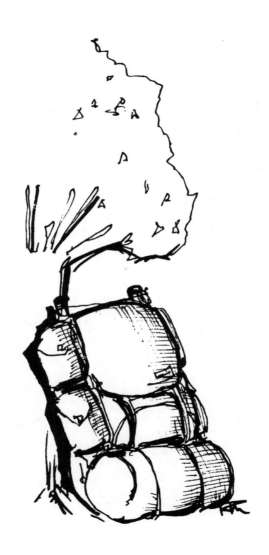